Preface

When Karl Marx died, his friend, Engles, eulogized the event, *"Mankind is shorter by a head, and by the most remarkable head of our time."*

Undoubtedly, Marxism is the most effective movement of our century. It is an explicit manifestation of what is implicit in Humanism—the ultimate realization of man as the measure of the universe. Under previous economic systems, Marx would argue, the masses of people had no hope of happiness on earth, so they sublimated their desires to an illusory paradise to come. Within the axiom of dialectical materialism, the apotheosis of communism, lies iconoclastic Humanism—that nothing exists beyond athiesm.

DEIRDRE MANIFOLD, in this piercing treatise, provides a twentieth century view of Karl Marx by unveiling the esoteric, sophistic, and cataclysmic global impact of this remarkable head; aptly named *"A Prophet Of Our Time."*

Publisher

ISBN 0-945001-00-2
Library of Congress 87-082937

G.S.G. & Associates
Publishers
P. O. Box 6448
Eastview Station
Rancho Palos Verdes, California 90734

This book is dedicated to my friend, John O'Connor, and to you who question, search, test, and apply discernment.

D.M.

Baroness Jenny von Westphalen

CONTENTS

CHAPTER 1

The Tavern Club, composed of students from Trier, met at the White Horse Inn at Godesberg in 1836. Marx is below the X.

Early Life

Karl Marx was born in Trier at half past one on the morning of 5 May, 1818. Though he came from a long line of Jewish Rabbis, he was baptised into the Protestant religion as his father, Heinrich, a lawyer, had converted to Protestantism shortly before Karl's birth. In doing so Heinrich's motives would have been more political than religious, having to do with his position as a lawyer.

Trier has the reputation of being the oldest town in Germany. Its origins are lost in the mists of antiquity. Flourishing under the Romans, it later came to ruins but rose and flourished again in the Middle Ages.

Its position at the extreme edge of German-speaking territory made it an intermediary between German and French culture.

It changed rulers from time to time, belonging at one time to the Holy Roman Empire, then to France, and back to Germany once again.

After the French Revolution, a stream of French *emigrés* poured into Trier as well as other frontier towns. It is then not surprising that Trier was a place where conspiracies were hatched and where there was much coming and going on political missions.

In 1793, Goethe came to Trier. The town has one striking characteristic, he wrote *"It claims that it possesses more religious buildings than any other place of the same size, for within its walls are churches and chapels and cloisters and colleges and buildings dedicated to the chivalrous and Religious Orders to say nothing of abbacies and Carthusian convents..."*

Having been French for two decades, Trier was awarded to Prussia at the Congress of Vienna. The pick of Prussian officialdom was sent to the Rhineland Provinces charged with the duty of respecting local idiosyncracies (among other things). The Government did much for historical research. The inhabitants of Trier were proud of the wealth of Roman remains in their town. There was a lively interest in archaology, ample sums for research being provided by the Government. And so the Trier of antiquity rose once more from the ruins.

Trier lived on the vine and did a flourishing business due to the tariff which came into force in 1818, the year of Karl's birth.

But in this more than comfortable setting, Karl's father, a lawyer and a Jew, had somewhat less freedom than he would have had under French rule. The Chairman of the Commission which carried out the transfer from French to Prussian authority described him as a *"learned, very industrious and thoroughly conscientious man"* and warmly recommended that he be taken over to the Prussian service.

To become more acceptable to the authorities, Hirschel ha-Levi Marx had himself baptized into the Protestant religion and became Heinrich Marx. Though his ancestors on his father's and his mother's side alike had been Rabbis as far back as the family tree can be traced, the changeover was no great wrench. No strong ties bound him either to the Synagogue or the Church. In a letter to Karl he once wrote that he received nothing from his family except, to be fair, "my mother's love."

On the 24th August 1824, Heinrich's children, Sophie, Karl, Hermann, Henriette, Louise, Emilie and Karoline were received into the Evangelical Church. Their mother, Henriette, waited until her parents were dead before being baptised on the 20th November 1825. Her maiden name was Pressburg and she came of a family of Hungarian origin which had been settled in Holland for generations. She was a devoted housewife, lovingly concerned for the minor things of life, engrossed in the health, feeding and clothing of her children.

Henriette would not appear to have understood her son, Karl. She never forgave him for not becoming a lawyer, like his father. She regarded his activities as suspicious, from an early age. Measured by her dreams about his future, a genius, maybe, but a failure, incompetent, the black sheep of the family.

Not much is known about Karl's brothers and sisters. The firstborn, Moritz David, died soon after birth. The next child Sophie, born on 13th November 1816, was the only one of Karl's brothers and sisters who was at all close to him in his youth. She married a lawyer named Schmalhansen and lived in Maastricht. Of Karl's two younger brothers, Hermann died at the age of 23 and Eduard at the age of eleven. Both died from tuberculosis, the hereditary family disease, as did two other sisters, Henriette and Karoline. Louise, born in 1821, married Jan Karl Juta, a Dutchman, and settled in Cape Town. She and her husband twice visited Marx in London. Emilie, born in 1822, married an engineer named Conradi and lived in Trier until her death in 1888.

Heinrich Marx was a lawyer attached to the Trier Court. He occupied a respected position in the social life of the town. The family lived in a beautiful old house in the Rhineland baroque style in the Bruckenstrasse, one of the best parts of the town. Trier was a small place. In 1818, when Marx was born, it numbered 11,400 inhabitants, of whom the overwhelming majority were Catholic. The Protestant community, to which the Marx's now belonged, consisted of barely 300 souls, mainly officials transferred to the Moselle from other provinces.

Towards the end of the 1820's, the condition of the peasants of the Moselle took a turn for the worse because of a customs union between Prussia and Hessia. Competition from non-Prussian wine-growing peasants caused prices to fall rapidly, to the accompaniment of rising taxes. Trade slumped. The peasants were pauperized. The position of the artisans went from bad to worse. The people became discontented. There was much unrest. Revolutionary ideas seeped in from France. Heinrich Marx made some imprudent speeches and as a result was regarded by the Government as thoroughly unreliable politically. Young Karl, then sixteen, was much concerned as he was deeply devoted to his father. Karl's daughter, Eleanor, recalled that he never tired of talking about him and always carried with him a photograph of him.

Very little is known about Marx's boyhood apart from some reminiscences by his sisters. They show him as an unruly companion at play. He seems to have been a fearful tyrant. He drove the girls at full gallop down the Marberg and insisted on their eating the cake he made with his dirty hands out of still dirtier dough. But they put up with it all without protest because he told them such marvellous stories in return. His schoolmates loved him and feared him at the same time — loved him because he was always up to tricks, and feared him because of the ease with which he wrote satirical verses and lampoons upon his enemies.

In 1830, at the age of 12, Karl went to High School. He was a moderate pupil. The best pupils were singled out at the end of each school year. Karl once received an "honourable mention" for ancient and modern languages but he was only tenth on the list, and another time was praised for his performance at German composition. He passed his examinations without distinction. He had the reputation among pupils and masters of being a poet. The essays he wrote at his final examination were clearly influenced by the French liberal intelligentia — and particularly by Rousseau. In an essay called **"Considerations of a young Man on choosing a career"** he says:

"If we choose the career in which we can do humanity the most good, burdens cannot overwhelm us since they are nothing but sacrifice for the benefit of all ...

"Experience rates him as the happiest who has made the greatest number happy, and religion itself teaches us the ideal for which all strive, to sacrifice oneself for humanity."

Karl's father was quite comfortably off and it was always understood within the family that Karl would go to University. However, Karl's younger brother, Hermann, had to be content with being indentured to a Brussels business house. Karl, the favorite child, was to be denied nothing.

Most students from Trier went to Bonn, the nearest

University town. When Karl went, there were thirty students from Trier there. It was intended that Karl should later go on to University in Berlin.

Bonn, a city or town of about 40,000 people, had then 700 students at the University. Indeed the University could be said to dominate the life of the town, and had boasted of the great freedom it enjoyed.

Karl went up, as one might say, in September 1835, and took a room quite close to the University. He seemed avid to learn everything and decided to take courses in no less than nine subjects. His father wrote *"Nine courses of lectures seem rather a lot to me, and I don't want you to undertake more than mind and body can stand, but if you can manage it, very well. The field of knowledge is immense and time is short."*

In the end, Marx attended six courses and was described as very industrious and exceptionally attentive. In the summer term he attended four courses. The year in Bonn was the only year in which he took his studies seriously. Later in Berlin he would only cover fourteen courses in nine terms.

He joined the Trier tavern club and was one of its five presidents in the summer of 1836. In June he was condemned to one day's detention by the Proctor for being drunk and disorderly. Karl joined another club called the "Poets' Club" of which he was an active member. His father approved of this as an outlet for Karl's stormy nature.

But what was Karl thinking about at this time? In **"The Union of the Faithful with Christ"** he writes: *"Through love of Christ we turn our hearts at the same time toward our brethren who are inwardly bound to us and for whom He gave Himself as a sacrifice."*[1] He continues: *"Union with Christ could give an inner elevation, comfort in sorrow, calm trust, and a heart susceptible to human love, to everything noble and great, not for the sake of ambition and glory, but only for the sake of Christ."* And in **"Considerations of a young Man on choosing a Career"** he writes: *"Religion itself teaches us that the Ideal toward which all strive sac-*

rifices Himself for humanity, and who shall dare contradict such claims? If we have chosen the position in which we can accomplish the most for Him, then we can never be crushed by burdens because they are only sacrifices made for the sake of all" and in **"The Capital"** he writes: *"Christianity with its cultus of abstract man, more especially in its bourgeois developments, Protestantism, Deism, etc., is the most fitting form of religion."*[2]

And under "Religious Knowledge", this was written of him in a certificate *"His knowledge of the Christian faith and morals is fairly clear and well grounded. He knows also to some extent the history of the Christian Church."*[3]

The summer and autumn of 1836 Karl spent in Trier where he became secretly engaged to Jenny Von Westphalen. Jenny's grandfather, Philip Westphalen (1724-92), was adviser and confidential secretary to Duke Ferdinand of Brunswick. He married Jenny Wishart of Pitharrow of the family of the Earls of Argyll, who played an important role in the history of Scotland.

Jenny had had a happy and carefree childhood. Her parents were rich. Ludwig Von Westphalen's salary in the early 1820's was 1,600 thalers a year, and in addition there was the income of a respectable estate, this at a time when 6 to 7 thalers a month could provide good furnished rooms, and a four-course dinner for a whole month could be had for seven thalers. The Westphalens occupied a sumptuous house with a big garden in one of the best streets in Trier. The Marx family lived next door. Jenny's favourite playmate was Karl's elder sister, Sophie. Edgar, a year younger than Karl, sat next to him on the same school bench. Westphalen himself, half-German, half-Scottish, had no national or racial prejudices. Lessing was one of his favourite authors. That Heinrich Marx had only recently become a Christian worried him not at all. The children made friends (the Marx children playing in the Westphalen garden) and the parents followed suit.

Jenny appeared to possess a rare beauty, to have been a

charming bewitching creature, the prettiest girl in Trier. Many could hardly understand how her choice could fall on Karl. In the autumn of 1836, he became secretly engaged to Jenny, but the secret was known to Karl's father, who reminded him of man's sacred duty to the weaker sex, and that if he persisted in his decision he must become a man at once.

In October Karl went to Berlin. In order to marry, it was necessary to complete his studies, pass his examinations and find a job. Karl was 18 and Jenny 22.

Karl was a poor correspondent, but he made up for his neglect of Jenny by sending her a volume of his poems, **The Book of Love,** dedicated to his dear ever-beloved Jenny Von Westphalen. Then at the end of 1837, Karl and Jenny became officially engaged.

STUDENT DAYS IN BERLIN

There were several thousand students in Berlin, a city of 300,000 souls, second only to Vienna in size and importance.

Karl matriculated in the faculty of Law on 22 October, 1837. In the first term he attended only three courses of lectures, on philosophy, on anthropology and on criminal law.

Here Karl was much influenced by Gans who, after the death of Hegel in 1831, lectured on history as well as law, the history of the French Revolution and its effects on the rest of Europe in particular. His lectures were attended not only by students but by officials, officers, men of letters — the whole of Berlin, in fact, everyone who was still concerned with political and social questions at that time.

The University was the one place where this could happen, as outside the University there was still censorship. Gans was one of the few who made real use of his academic freedom. He expressed opinions and praised the French Revolution in his lectures in a way he could not possibly have done outside the University. Karl listened with great zeal and Gan's report on him was that he was "exceptionally industrious."

While studying law Karl felt an urge to wrestle with philosophy, as he felt that without philosophy nothing very much could be accomplished. He studied English and Italian in order *'once more to search for the dance of the Muse and the music of the satyrs.'*

His father had been giving him 700 thalers a year. This was an enormous sum at the time, more than double the annual income of most families. Karl's father died in 1838 when Karl was twenty. During that last year the family's material position had been worsening, yet Karl was always asking for more money. Also he does not appear to have been doing much work at his studies. He had joined the Doktors' Klub, a group of coffee house graduates who spent long hours debating, mostly the ideas of Hegel. A friend of his in the Klub, Bruno Bauer, urged him to put a stop to his shillyshallying and to end his *'wearisome vacillation about the sheer, nonsensical farce of his examinations.'* He was urged to go to Bonn, where he would find things easy. At Bonn he would be able to get a lectureship. The Professors at Bonn knew they were no philosophers and that the students wanted to hear philosophy. From Bonn Bruno wrote *"Come here and the new battle will begin."*

On 30 March, 1841 Karl received his leaving certificate from Berlin. A week later, on April 6th he sent to Jena his dissertation on **"The Difference between the Natural Philosophies of Democrites and the Epicureans"**[4] *"Certain negotiations appear to have preceded this step. The University of Jena was celebrated at the time for the readiness with which it granted doctors' degrees. It lived up to its reputation, for a week later the Dean of Jena University presented the candidate, Karl Heinrich Marx, to the faculty of philosophy. The diploma was dated the 15th April. Karl's official student years were at an end."*[5]

Robert Payne, author of an excellant biography of Marx,

has commented on his years at University; *'There was, of course, nothing particularly unusual in such a University career. In all the Universities of Germany there were always students who attended few lectures, piled up debts, and frittered their lives away. So it had been since the Middle Ages and so it would continue. These students had invented a special jargon, and their own Bohemian uniform. They were part of the University and outside it. They belonged to the no man's land where eccentricities breed and culture goes to seed."*[6]

In 1842 Karl got his first job on the newly established *Rheinische Zeitung,* having already been a regular contributor. He was recommended for the job by Moses Hess. After a few months the paper was closed down and Karl was out of a job.

In 1843 Karl decided it was time to end his seven year courtship of Jenny, and on June 13th they were married. The young couple spent a few months at the Westphalen's house in Kreuznach. While there a friend of Karl's father offered him a job in the Government. This he refused.

The long honeymoon was spent on a tour through Switzerland where, Jenny later related, they literally gave money away, Jenny's mother having given the couple a small legacy for the trip. Karl spent much time reading and writing. At the end of October the couple went to Paris, where Karl was to edit another paper; however, the paper ceased after one issue.

His next few years were spent in study, in writing and meetings with revolutionary groups, the most notable being The League of the Just, a highly secret society at whose behest he would later write **The Communist Manifesto.**

In January 1845, Marx went to Brussels from whence he was expelled in March 1848. He then moved on to Cologne where he began the publication of the *Neue Rheinische Zeitung,* but this landed him in Court, being acquitted on a charge of subversion. In May he left for France, but was expelled three months later. From there he went to Switzerland, the home of most 19th century radicals of the time. From there he was to go to London, which was to be home for himself and his family for the rest of his life.

It was in London that he was to gain the reputation of living in great poverty, even squalor. This does not mean that he had no money. He went through vast sums while subjecting his family to the most awful privation. In London three of his children died, due, no doubt, in part, to such harsh living conditions. As he had mastered several European languages he could easily have made a good living for his family, and still have had time for his writing. Only once when Engels failed to come to the rescue did Karl look for a job with the Railway Company, but he failed to get it owing to his bad handwriting.[7] He had a small regular income from The New York Daily Tribune, to which he submitted regular articles.

Jenny left some unfinished autobiographical notes, set down in the mid '60's but not published for nearly a century, in which she mused: *"Why did I see my children die from hunger?"*

Their poverty could be said to be of the genteel kind, for when Mrs. Marx was pregnant with Laura in April, 1845, she received from her mother, the widowed Baroness von Westphalen, *"the best present she could send her, dear faithful, Lenchen."* Lenchen, also known as Helene Demuth, was 22 years old. She had grown up as a servant girl with the Westphalen family, so that when she rejoined her young mistress she had only been briefly separated from her. From then on Lenchen was to share all the ups and downs of the Marx family, flitting with them from one country to another. Children were born and children died. Helene's wages were seldom paid, her few belongings as often in the pawn as those of the Marx's. She was to be the one constant in the Marx family. She ordered and sustained the whole household, baking bread, making and patching clothes, mending shoes, washing linen, and brewing beer.

On 23rd June, 1851, Helene gave birth to a son, Henry

Frederick Demuth, who was put out to foster parents. Deprived of the rearing of her own child (fathered by Karl), Helene lavished all her affection on Karl's youngest daughter, Eleanor. For many years a pretence was kept up that her child had been fathered by Engels in order to save Karl embarrassment. Henry Frederick became Karl's only male issue. Not much seems to be known about the day to day living of the family while on mainland Europe, but their years in London are well recorded.

1 Marx & Engels Collected Works, Vol. I, International Publishers, N.Y. (1974).
2 "The Capital". Chapter I, Section IV.
3 Archive for the History of Socialism and the Workers' Movement, 1925 in German.
4 MEGA. I, I/I pp 3-144.
5 Karl Marx, Man & Fighter, Boris Nicolaievsky and Otto Maenchen-Helfen, Penguin Books. P. 45.
6 Robert Payne, Marx, Simon & Schuster, 1968. pp 78-9.
7 Letters to Kugelman, International Publishers, 1934. P. 24.

CHAPTER 2

9 Grafton Terrace, Maitland Park, Haverstock Hill, where Marx lived
from 1856 to 1864.

The London Years

When the Marx family came to London they settled at 28
Dean St., in the Borough of Westminster. Three of their
children died there, one an eight year old boy, Henry
Edgar. The rent at Dean St. was £22 per annum, not
always paid by Karl.

On 16 January, 1855, Karl's youngest daughter, Eleanor,
was born. Karl remarked at the time that if it had been a
male the *"matter would have been more acceptable"*, yet
Tussy, as this child came to be known, was to
become his favourite.

In the following year, 1856, Mrs. Marx took her three
daughters to Trier where her mother, the Baroness von
Westphalen, lay ill. There they remained for three months.
Jenny was to inherit about £120 from her mother, and in
the same year, 1856, according to a letter Mrs. Marx wrote
to Mrs. Markheim, a friend of the family, she inherited
almost £200 from a Scottish relative.

With the change of fortune the family made
arrangements to leave Soho, moving to No. 9 Grafton Tce.,
Kentish Town. Some of their debts were paid off, though
not all, for it is recorded that three years later the Dean
St. milkman and baker were owed the substantial sum of
£9.[1] The rent was £36 a year, rateable valuation, £27, with
rates £2.3.10d. The family were to remain there for more
than seven years. During that time Mrs. Marx recalled:
*"We were permanently hard up, our debts mounted from day
to day."*[2] Engels had agreed to pay the family £5 a month.
This was rapidly stepped up as one crisis followed another,
and in response to Marx's plea that the hand-to-mouth
existence of Dean Street was no longer feasible for a
householder and ratepayer with three daughters to bring
up, the two older girls, Laura and Jenny, being now
enrolled in the South Hampstead College for Ladies at
Clarence House, 18 Haverstock Hill, where the fees were
£8 a term, with extra fees for languages and drawing. *"And
now I have to engage a music fellow"*, Karl wrote to Engels
in April, 1857.[3] He sent him a detailed account of his

debts amounting to £113 owed to the local butcher, baker, grocer, milkman, greengrocer and news-agent, the last not having been paid for a twelvemonth. *"Even if I were to reduce my expenses to the utmost"*, Karl wrote *"by, for example, removing the children from school, going to live in a strictly working-class dwelling, dismissing the servants and living on potatoes"*, the sale of the furniture would not realise enough to satisfy the creditors, while such drastic steps where hardly suitable for his growing girls.[4]

Engels came to the rescue, as he did again and again, not only with cash but also with crates of wine, regarded as an unfailing remedy for every bodily ill.

The family may have considered that they lived in terrible discomfort, but with their two maids and fine house they did in fact live in luxury compared to the other refugees who swarmed into the Soho part of London following the 1848 Revolution. They came from France, Poland, Russia, Italy and Germany — a human tide that did not recede for a decade. They lived in the alleys of Leicester Square, and the adjoining backstreets .... a wretched lot of miserable, poverty-stricken, harassed people.

Though 1859 was a tough year for the family, Christmas was celebrated with champagne sent by Engels. Also, in the late summer of that year the family went for two weeks to Hastings. Whenever the bailiffs were at the door, a timely cheque from Engels would arrive to settle the outstanding bills.

In 1861, having had just such a skirmish with his creditors, Karl prepared to go to Holland where he remained from March till May. Lion Philips, a successful businessman in Zalthommel, near Nijmegen, married to Karl's Aunt Sophie, managed the affairs of Karl's mother, herself of Dutch origin. The Philips family founded the firm of Philips Lamps, Ltd. in Eindhoven in 1891. Karl hoped for an advance. He travelled widely, going to Prussia, Germany, The Low Countries, and came home with £160, as well as laying the groundwork for contributing regular articles to the *Vienna Presse*. While he was away Engels, as usual, took financial care of the family.

According to Yvonne Kapp in her life of Eleanor, *"Keeping up appearances meant most to Marx where his daughters were concerned. He might rail against his wife's mild pretensions as false and pernicious, as 'roasting him over a slow fire', yet he shared her aspirations for the girls, and took offence at any suggestion that they should attempt to earn their living, for which, in however restricted a field, their polite studies might be thought to have equipped them ... that they might become self-supporting he looked upon as a mortification outweighing any to which they were daily and hourly exposed .... Marx treated as an impertinence Lassalle's well-intentioned proposal that they should go to Berlin as companions to the Countess Hatzfeldt .... Even training for a profession was unthinkable."*[5]

In the late summer of 1862 Jenny took the three girls to Ramsgate for three weeks. While they were away Karl paid another visit to his uncle in Zalthommel and to Trier. Their happy reunion was somewhat marred by the mounting debts, the butcher alone being owned £6 and no money in the house. Engels as usual came to the rescue, while Mrs. Bertha Markeim sent three separate Money Orders, one for £6.

1863 was a bad year for Karl, the American Civil War reducing his income from the U.S. somewhat. Engels was bereaved by the death of Mary Burns on January 6, 1863; nevertheless he sent Karl £100. There was a further remittance from Mrs. Markheim. In the summer Jenny and the girls went to Hastings, accompanied by their music teacher. Then on 30th November, 1863 news came that Karl's mother had died. Contacting Engels, he wrote: *"Two hours ago a telegram arrived to say that my mother had died. Fate needed to take one member of the family. I already had one foot in the grave. Under the circumstances, I am needed more than the old woman. I have to go to Trier about the inheritance.'*[6]

From Trier Karl travelled to Frankfort to see his aunts, Esther Kosel and Babette Blum, and finally to Zalthommel to settle the formalities of his mother's will with Lion Philips, her executor. He stayed in Holland nearly two months, by which time he received his inheritance of some £750, returning to London in February, 1864. On May 9th, at age 55, Wilhelm Wolff died. Marx became the main beneficiary, receiving £750. Wolff had been a member of the League of the Just who had commissioned Karl to write the **Manifesto.**

With the aid of the two legacies the family made immediate arrangements to move house, this time to No. 1, Modena Villas, Maitland Park, spending £500 on the move. In the summer there were holidays in Brighton and Ramsgate for all the family. In October the girls gave a ball for 50 young people. It was such a lavish affair that next day Tussy was able to have an impromptu children's party with the left-overs. Incredible as it may seem, less than a year later the legacies had all vanished. Mrs. Marx had to appeal to Engels for money while Marx was away in Holland. The tide of debts flowed back, accompanied by the usual round of pawning and borrowing.

The high standard of living however had its advantages. The girls were able to meet the right people, the two older ones being of marriageable age. Already a French medical student, named Paul Lafargue, showed an interest in Laura. His parents owned a prosperous wine business in Bordeaux. He had studied at the University of Paris, but because of his revolutionary activity was excluded from the University. He hoped to take his finals in Strasbourg. Soon he proposed to Laura. Mrs. Marx related the good news to Engels, who sent an extra £50 over and above the £200 a year he had been sending regularly. The engagement was formally announced on 26 September, 1866, Laura's 21st birthday. Mrs. Marx was overjoyed and in a letter to a friend, Ernestine Liebnecht, let it be known that his parents had considerable estates in Cuba and had established a prosperous wine business in Bordeaux. Paul had acquitted himself brilliantly at the University, taking his B.M. degree with honours after four years' study. Also she did not forget to add that, fortunately, he would not be dependent on his practice, always so precarious at the start, as his parents were well-off, owning plantations and house property in Santiago and Bordeaux, and as Paul was their only child, all would pass on to him. The family had behaved capitally towards Laura, welcoming her as their daughter with open arms, promising a gift of 100,000 frs. on their wedding day (roughly £4,000). And she added: *"What I consider quite a remarkable piece of luck is that he has the same principles, in particular where religion is concerned; thus Laura will be spared the inevitable conflicts and sufferings to which any girl with her opinions is exposed in society. For how rare it is nowadays to find a man who shares such views and at the same time has culture and a social position .... I always thought Laura would be a lucky girl ...."* Laura's marriage took place on April 2, 1868 at St. Pancras Registry Office. The honeymoon was spent in Paris, where her father sent Laura a letter asking her to send him some catalogs and journals, adding, *"I am a machine, condemned to devour books and then throw them up, in a changed form, on the dunghill of history."*[7]

1867 was a busy year for Karl as the first volume of **Das Kapital** was sent to the Publishers in Germany, but he had other problems too of another kind. No. 1 Modena Villas changed ownership, and the new owner made it clear from the start he meant business in the matter of collection when the due date came round by holding a pistol to Karl's head, for the rent was disgracefully in arrears.

Karl left London on 6th April and was away for about six weeks. Engels sent £35 and a note for the publisher to pay Marx some money owed by the firm on his own work. Engels also provided for the family while Marx was away.

Engels was due to go abroad in July. He sent £100 before leaving. The three girls had been invited to spend a holiday in Bordeaux with Paul's family, where they stayed for a few months.

On 14 September, 1867, the first edition of Vol. 1 of **Das Kapital** was published, the result of ten years work. Prospects were becoming distinctly brighter in 1868, with Laura married and settled in Paris, and Engels made arrangements to wind up his business affairs in Manchester. He required to know from Karl how much he actually owed and, if he would be able to make a clean start free of debt, did he think he could live on £350 a year — illness and other unforeseen contingencies apart — for this was the regular income Engels proposed to guarantee him, to start in 1869; and so on 1 January, 1869, the first quarterly installment of this regular private income was deposited for Karl at the Union Bank of London. Another joyful event was the announcement of the birth of Laura's son, Charles Etienne Lafargue. And as if this were not enough great news, Jenny, determined to earn her own keep, went and got herself a job. Now there was only Eleanor to provide for.

That spring there were holidays in Paris for both Eleanor and Jenny, and as Paul Lafargue had finished his translation of **The Communist Manifesto,** Jenny took it back with her to London. Eleanor stayed on for many weeks, savouring the joys of seeing Paris.

The following year, 1870, Engels moved to London, taking up residence at 122 Regent's Park Road, where he was to live for the next 24 years.

The next big event to occur in the family was Jenny's engagement to the Frenchman, Charles Longuet. Longuet was born in Caen in 1839, had been a former fellow student of Lafargue, and, like Lafargue, was a member of the radical movement in Paris. The marriage took place at St. Pancras Registry Office on 9 October, 1872. They then went to live in Oxford where Longuet hoped to teach

French. Eleanor, now aged 17, became engaged to yet another Frenchman, the dashing, flamboyant, Lissagaray, one of the Commune's most outstanding fighters: he, however, did not find favour with either Karl or his wife. They never recognized the engagement, and though it lasted for nine years, it eventually fizzled out, since Karl would not give his consent to the marriage.

Their judgment in the matter of sons-in-law would not appear to have been very sound, for though both Lafargue and Longuet came from wealthy families, and had received a first-class education, they both failed to support their families and shamelessly sponged on Engels. Eventually Eleanor, Karl's favourite, and the pet of the family, went to live with Edward Aveling, a by no means reputable character, and from whom she parted at the early age of 43 by committing suicide. The union would appear to have had Karl's approval.

Mrs. Marx did not think too highly of Frenchmen for she wrote in a letter to friend Liebnecht, in May, 1872: *"I had sincerely hoped that Jenny's choice, for a change, would have fallen on an Englishman, or a German rather than a Frenchman, who, combined with the national qualities of charm is naturally not without their weakness and irresponsibility,"* and again *"if one does not choose to believe their pack of lies and French fiddledeedee which I find impossible to do, one is considered a 'Prussian' "*.

Later that summer Mrs. Marx had other things to worry about, for Laura's only surviving child died early in July. The Lafargues at the time were refugees in Spain from recently war-torn France. There was also the Hague Congress of the International to be attended by Marx, a matter of life and death to him.

By the following spring Eleanor had found herself employment, teaching in Brighton, for which the pupils paid her 10s. a week. Pining for her beloved Lissagaray, she wrote her father the following letter dated 23 March 1874:

"My dearest Mohr,

I am going to ask you something, but first I want you to promise me that you will not be very angry. I want to know, dear Mohr, when I may see L. again. It is so very hard never to see him. I have been doing my best to be patient but it is so difficult and I don't feel as if I could be much longer. I do not expect you to say that he can come here. I should not even wish it, but could I not now and then, go for a little walk with him ... No one more-over will be astonished to see us together, as everybody knows we are engaged .... Believe me, dear Mohr, if I could see him now and then it would do me more good than all Mrs. Anderson's prescriptions put together .... I know that by experience.

At any rate, dearest Mohr, if I may not see him now, could you not say **when** *I may. It would be something to look forward to, and if the time were not so indefinite it would be less wearisome to wait.*

My dearest Mohr, please don't be angry with me for writing this, but forgive me for being selfish enough to worry you again.

Yours, Tussy

P.S. This is quite entre nous."[8]

How times have changed, and who has done more to bring about such changes in bringing up a family than Karl Marx!

Despite the fact that Eleanor's pleas to her stern father fell on deaf ears, it did not appear to affect their friendship, for in the summer of 1874 we find the two of them setting out for Carlsbad to take the waters as a cure-all for all ailments. Before going, Karl decided to apply for British nationality and was turned down. He went nevertheless, though he feared arrest. All the best people were there, kings and queens, priests and noblemen, famous writers and musicians, including Beethoven and Paganini, while Turgenev spent June of the same year there.

With such company around there was naturally no lack of social life, where much laughter and little thought were prescribed. Here Karl and daughter enjoyed all the benefits of the bourgeois life he had set out to destroy. Here was a life about as far removed as it could be from that of the working class of England, or indeed of any country, and Karl and Eleanor loved it. After the usual few weeks there they set out for Leipzig. From there they went to Berlin and then on to Hamburg where Karl discussed his affairs with his publisher, coming back to England at the beginning of October.

By the end of 1874 the Lafargues and the Longuets had come to live in London, Jenny's husband having been appointed assistant Master in French at King's College in the University of London at a salary of £180 a year, while Jenny herself began teaching German at St. Clement Dane's School in Stanhope St.

The following year in March, 1875, the family moved to 41 Maitland Park Road, a smaller house, yet a substantial one, more than adequate for four people. In September we find Karl in Carlsbad again, this time minus Eleanor, while Mrs. Marx went to Lausanne.

Again in 1876 Karl and Eleanor were off to Carlsbad from the middle of August to the middle of September. En route Karl paid a nostalgic visit to Kreusnach where he had been married in 1843. The Westphalen family had travelled from Triers *"preferring that reactions to this unpopular event should not be manifested in their home town."*[9]

About this time Marx had more than his share of family problems. Paul Lafargue having given up the effort to qualify in medicine had set up as a commercial photo-engraver which must not have been all that successful, since he seemed to think that Engels owed him, as well as his father-in-law, a living. There were also problems with the Longuet family, forcing Jenny out to work to make ends meet despite a persistent asthmatic cough. Longuet being of

an irritable nervous temper was not easy to live with, and to
make matters worse an equally irritable mother of his spent
much time with them.

The years rolled by. Karl and his wife were beginning to
feel the stress of the years on their health. Mrs. Marx com-
plained of pain. It was decided she should go at once to
Manchester to see one Dr. Gumpert, a friend of the family.
There while receiving medical attention she managed quite
a social round, going to a Halle concert and even attending
a Roman Catolic Church to hear the music. Mrs. Marx could
be detached and humorous enough to say about her health
that the head and feet were all right but that the centre of
the machine where the brewing takes place was not yet in
working order.

Things did not improve for her, for the following year we
find her in Malvern seeking a cure. There, she felt that if
she had come earlier she would have had a better chance of
a cure. While there she invited Jenny to come and stay, as
she had had quite a hard time since her marriage. Two of
her little boys had died. She now had a little boy and a girl.
Eleanor was deputed to mind the little boy while she was
away. Living with Longuet was no bed of roses, it being
necessary to go out to teach, and then her mother-in-law
seems to have been a constant source of irritation. Now she
wanted her son back in France where his property was
being sequestrated, running her into losses amounting to
millions of francs. An amnesty was awaited for all those
1870 Communards. This both Karl and Mrs. Marx awaited
with mixed feelings for they dreaded the loss of their
grandchildren and of course their children. Later Karl was
to write to Jenny, a month after she left for France: *"I often
run to the window when I hear children's voices .... forgetting
for the moment that the little fellows are across the chan-
nel."*[10]

Mrs. Marx's condition worsened. As she weakened she
longed to see her grandchildren again, insisting on a visit to
France, which Karl thought out of the question. He took her

instead to Eastbourne for three weeks. Upon her return however, her doctor, one Dr. Donkin, having examined her, allowed her to travel; so on 26 July 1881 she, with Karl and Lenchen, left for France to stay with the Longuets at 11 Boulevard Thiers in Argenteuil. News that Eleanor was ill in London broke up the French visit sooner than intended. Karl left by himself, Mrs. Marx and Lenchen following in easier stages. As the year wore on, her condition worsened and then to make matters worse Karl developed pleurisy, with only Eleanor and Lenchen to nurse them both. Eleanor recalled after: *"our mother lay in the large front room, Mohr in the little room behind. And the two of them who were so used to one another, so close to one another, could not be together in the same room .... Never shall I forget the morning when he felt strong enough to go into mother's room. When they were together they were young again — she a loving girl and he a loving youth, on the threshold of life, not an old man devastated by illness and an old woman parting from each other for life."*

Eleanor was to write to Jenny, 4 December 1881[11] that during the last month when her mother *"suffered all the tortures that cancer brings with it .... her good humour, her inexhaustible wit .... never deserted her for an instant. She inquired as impatiently as a child for the results of the elections then being held in Germany .... Up to her death she remained cheerful and tried to expel our anxiety by joking. Yes, in spite of her fearful suffering she joked — she laughed — she laughed at the doctor and all of us because we were so serious. She remained fully conscious almost until the last moment, and when she could no longer speak .... she pressed our hands and tried to smile, but the last word she spoke was to Papa!* "Good" Eleanor added that she rejoiced she had made the journey to Paris and relived the happiness it had given her and that to the very end she thought of herself and the children more than of anyone.

Mrs. Marx was not quite 68 years old when she died on 2 December, 1881. She was buried in Highgate cemetery near her first-born grandson, Charles Longuet. Karl was as yet unable to go out so he could not attend. Engels was to say at the burial: *"If ever there was a woman whose greatest happiness lay in making others happy, this was she."*[12]

When it was all over Eleanor wrote to Jenny, sending her a piece of her mother's *"dear hair .... as soft and beautiful as a girl's"* — recalling the *"sweet expression as she saw and recognized us, which she did at the end."*[13]

In a family where there was so much conversation between all the members it is difficult to understand what Eleanor had to say later in a letter to Olive Schreiner, 16 June 1884, quoted in Adelphi, Havelock Ellis' New Series, Vol. 6. 1935: *"My mother and I loved each other passionately .... One of the bitterest sorrows of my life is that my mother died, thinking, despite all our love, that I had been hard and cruel, and never guessing that to save her and father I had sacrificed the best, freshest years of my life."* When it came to misunderstandings it seems the Marx family was no different from so many others.

Early in February 1882, we find Karl and Eleanor in France visiting Jenny. He stayed there for a week before setting out for Algiers. He was to stay there and in the South of France until June. Eleanor had by now broken off her engagement to Lissagaray. Nevertheless he called and saw her off at the Gare St. Lazare when she set out for home. Jenny was glad the engagement had ended, saying that French husbands were not worth much at the best of times — and at the worst — well, the less said the better. In a letter on 7 March, 1882 to Eleanor she said *"These Frenchmen at the best of times make pitiable husbands."*

The sojourn in Algiers did nothing much to improve Karl's health. He came back via Monte Carlo staying at the Hotel de Russie from early May until early June, when he returned to Paris to the home of Jenny. He stayed there for three months enjoying very much home life with his grandchildren. What he needed, he told Jenny, was the microscopic world of children's noises. Lenchen was there too, and Eleanor came later in the summer. Laura too changed house from London to Paris that same summer. Jenny was expecting another baby, needing all the family help she could get.

That Karl realised the seriousness of the state of his health is clear from a letter to Engels in which he said *"Naturally, at a certain age, it is altogether a matter of indifference how one is 'launched into eternity'. "* When Eleanor arrived in Paris she was dismayed at his changed appearance. That he was afraid to travel alone he confided to Laura, asking her to accompany him to Switzerland at the end of August. When they returned, Jenny had given birth to a daughter.

Karl arrived back in London in the first week of October. At the end of the month, warned not to remain in London during the season of damp and fog, Karl set off for Ventnor. Eleanor kept in constant touch with him by letter. He was to remain in the Isle of Wight until the spring, but this was not to be.

Family trouble was looming in the shape of Jenny's health. She was suffering from inflammation of the bladder, which she tried to conceal from her father. And as if that weren't enough, Paul Lafargue was summoned to appear before the magistrate's court to show reason why he should not stand trial for subversive speeches he and others had made. His failure to comply was followed by his arrest on 12 December. Laura immediately summoned Engels to come to the rescue, which as usual he did promptly.

Lenchen was to go to France to look after Jenny. Things moved to a head so quickly, before she could leave, word came that Jenny had died on the afternoon of 11 January 1883. She was not quite 39 years old.

It was left to Eleanor to bring the news to Karl. In later years Eleanor recalled that she felt she was bringing him his death sentence. *"On the long journey I tortured my brain thinking how to impart the news to him .... my face betrayed it. Mohr said at once 'Our Jenny is dead', I have lived many a sad hour, but none so sad as that."* Karl urged her there and then to go to France to help with Jenny's children and *"would not suffer any contradiction",* though Eleanor felt she would have preferred to stay with him in his unutterable grief at the death of his first-born — the daughter he loved most, as he was wont to say.

Karl himself returned immediately to London; he had come home to die. Jenny's death was the last terrible blow. He suffered a series of spasmodic attacks. He had attacks of asthma, laryngitis and bronchitis. His voice was hoarse and he found it hard to swallow. In February he developed a tumour of the lung.

His tug of war with life was nearly over. Nursed by Eleanor and the ever-faithful Lenchen, Karl died suddenly and peacefully on 14 March 1883 at two o'clock in the afternoon. He was 65 years old. He was buried on 17 March in the same grave as his wife. A week later it was reopened to receive the remains of four and a half year old Harry Longuet, whom Eleanor had brought over from France as she returned to the bedside of her father. Engels was to write of the event: *"mankind is shorter by a head and by the most remarkable head of our time."*

1 Eleanor Marx, by Yvonne Kapp P.30, Lawrence & Sishart 1972.
2 *Ibid* P.30
3 *Ibid* P.32
4 *Ibid* P.35
5 *Ibid* P.42
6 Letter 2/12/1863 MEW XXX 376
7 11 April 1868. Original English MIML.
8 Bottigelli Archives
9 Kapp.
10 Kapp. P.216
11 Bottigelli Archives 7 October 1881.
12 Published in *L'Egalite* on 11 December 1881.
13 Bottigelli Archives, Eleanor to Jenny, 4/12/1881.

CHAPTER 3

Paul Lafargue

Dr. Edward Aveling

Karl's Beliefs

Karl Marx was raised as a Christian. It is on record that when he finished the gymnasium the following was written under the heading "Religious Knowledge".: *"His knowledge of the Christian faith and morals is fairly clear and well grounded. He knows also to some extent the history of the Christian church."*[1]

His first written work is called **"The Union of the Faithful with Christ"** in which we find these words: *"Through love of Christ we turn our hearts at the same time towards our brethren who are inwardly bound to us and for whom He gave himself as a sacrifice."*[2] And in an essay called **"Considerations of a young Man choosing a Career"** we read:

If we choose the career in which we can do humanity the most good, burdens cannot overwhelm us, since they are nothing but sacrifice for the good of all .... Experience rates him as the happiest who has made the greatest number happy, and religion itself teaches us the ideal for which all strive, to sacrifice oneself for humanity.[3]

Very soon after receiving his school certificate something strange happened to him. All of a sudden he seems to have set his mind against all religion in a profound and passionate way. He writes in a poem *"I wish to avenge myself against the one who rules above"* thus showing that he believed there is one above who rules, and he was in a quarrel with him. Why? It is hard to fathom. The One above had done him no wrong. Karl belonged to a relatively well-to-do family. He was much better off than most of his fellow students, and they in turn were far better off than most. Why the passionate hatred of God? Why the following lines in his poem **"Invocation of One in Despair"**?

So a god has snatched from me my all
In the curse and rack of destiny
All his worlds are gone beyond recall!
Nothing but revenge is left to me,
I shall build my throne high overhead,
Cold, tremendous shall its summit be,

> *For its bulwark — superstitious dread,*
> *For its Marshall — blackest agony.*[4]

Why should any young man with such bright prospects in life want to build a throne from which would emanate dread and agony? Does this not remind one of Lucifer's boast: *"I will ascend into heaven, I will exalt my throne above the stars of God."*[5]

Why does Karl wish such a throne? The answer may be found in his poem **Oulanem** written while he was a student. Before quoting from the poem the following explanation is needed for an understanding of its contents.

There exists a Satanist Church. One of the rituals is the Black Mass, which a Satanist priest recites at midnight. Black candles are put in the candlesticks upside down. The priest is dressed in his ornate robes, but with the lining outside. He says all the things prescribed in the prayer-book, but reads from the end towards the beginning. The holy names of God, Jesus and Mary are read inversely. A crucifix is fastened upside down or trampled upon. The body of a naked woman serves as an altar. A consecrated host stolen from some church is inscribed with the name "Satan" and is used for a mock-Communion. During the Black Mass a Bible is burned. All those present promise to commit the seven deadly sins, as enumerated in the Catholic Catechism, and never to do any good. An orgy follows.

Devil worship is very old. We read in Deuteronomy 32:17 that the Jews "sacrificed unto devils". Later, King Jeroboam of Israel ordained priests for the devils.[6]

"Oulanem" is an inversion of Emmanuel, a Biblical name for Jesus, which means in Hebrew "With us is God". Such inversions of names are considered effective in black magic. We can better understand the drama Oulanem in the light of a strange confession which Marx made in a poem called **The Prayer,** later down-played by both himself and his followers:

> *The hellish vapours rise and fill the brain,*
> *Till I go mad and my heart is utterly changed.*

See this sword?
The prince of darkness
Sold it to me,
For he beats the time and gives the signs,
Ever more boldly I play the dance of death.[7]

In the rites of higher initiation into the Satanist cult an 'enchanted' sword which ensures success is sold to the candidate. He pays for it by signing a covenant, with blood taken from his wrists, that his soul will belong to Satan after death. Here then are some lines from the drama **Oulanem:**

And they are also Oulanem, Oulanem,
The name rings forth like death, rings forth
Until it dies away in a wretched crawl,
Stop, I've got it now! It rises from my soul
As clear as air, as strong as my own bones.
Yet I have power within my youthful arms
To clench and crush you (i.e. personified humanity) with
tempestuous force,
While for us both the abyss yawns in darkness,
You will sink down and I will follow laughing,
Whispering in your ears, "Descend, come with me
friend,"[8]

The Bible, which Marx had studied in his high school and which he knew quite well in his mature years, says that the devil will be bound by an angel and cast into the bottomless pit (*abyssos* in Greek: see Revelation 20:3). Marx wishes to draw the whole of mankind into this pit reserved for the devil and his angels. Who speaks through Marx in this drama? It is hardly reasonable to expect a young student to entertain as his life's dream the vision of mankind entering the abyss of darkness ("outer darkness" is a Biblical name for "hell") and himself laughing as he follows those he has led to unbelief. Nowhere in the world is this ideal cultivated except in the initiation rites of the Satanist church, at its highest degrees.

The time comes for Oulanem's death. His words are:

Ruined, ruined. My time has clean run out.
The clock has stopped, the pygmy house has crumbled,
Soon I shall embrace eternity to my breast, and soon
I shall howl gigantic curses on mankind.[9]

Karl had loved the words of Mephistopheles in **Faust,** *"Everything in existence is worth being destroyed."* Everything, including the proletariat and the comrades. Marx quoted these words in **The 18th Brumaire.**[10] Stalin acted on them and destroyed even his own family.

The Satanist sect is not materialistic. It believes in eternal life. Oulanem, the person for whom Marx speaks, does not deny eternal life. He asserts it, but as a life of hate magnified to its extreme. Eternity for the devils means torment. Thus Jesus was reproached by the demons: *"Art you come hither to torment us before our time?"* (Matthew 8:29). And too with Marx:

Ha! Eternity! She is our eternal grief
An indescribable and unmeasurable Death,
Vile artificiality conceived to scorn us,
Ourselves being clockwork, blindly mechanical,
Made to be the fool-calendars of Time and Space,
Having no purpose save to happen, to be ruined,
so that there shall be something to ruin.[11]

We can now see what was happening to young Karl. He had had Christian convictions but had not led a consistent life. His correspondence with his father shows that he was squandering great sums of money on pleasures, and that he was constantly quarrelling with his family about this and other matters. He may have fallen in with the tenets of the highly secret Satanist church and received the rites of initiation. Satan, whom his worshippers see in their hallucinatory orgies, speaks through them. Thus Marx is only Satan's mouthpiece when he utters in his poem **Invocation of One in Despair** the words, *"I wish to avenge myself against the One who rules above."* Hear the end of **Oulanem:**

If there is something which devours,
I'll leap within it, though I bring the world to ruins.

The world which bulks between me and the abyss
I will smash to pieces with my enduring curses.
I'll throw my arms around its harsh reality:
Embracing me, the world will dumbly pass away,
and sink down to utter nothingness,
Perished, with no existence — that would be really
living."

In **Oulanem** Marx does what the devil does: he consigns the entire human race to damnation. It is the only drama in the world in which all the characters are aware of their own corruption, which they flaunt and celebrate with conviction.

There is no black and white, no Claudius and Ophelia, all are black and reveal aspects of Mephistopheles. All are satanic, corrupt and doomed. Karl was only eighteen when he wrote these lines. And in a letter to his father he writes *"A curtain had fallen. My holy of holies was rent asunder and new gods had to be installed."* These words were written on 10 November 1837, by a young man who had professed Christianity until then. His father replies, *"I refrained from insisting on any explanation about a very mysterious matter although it seemed highly dubious."* On 2 March 1837, his father had written: *"Your advancement, the dear hope to see your name being one of great repute, and your earthly well-being are not the only desires of my heart. These are illusions I had had a long time, but I can assure you that their fulfilment would not have made me happy. Only if your heart remains pure and beats humanly and **if no demon** will be able to alienate your heart from better feelings, only then will I be happy."* The father is clearly unhappy about his son and fears demonic influence, and with good reason. The following is from Karl's poem **On Hegel:**

Words I teach all mixed up into a devilish muddle,
Thus anyone may think just what he chooses to think.

And in his poem **The Pale Maiden,** he writes:

Thus heaven I've forfeited,
I know it full well,
My soul, once true to God,

Is chosen for hell.

It is Karl who says it.

Karl's favourite child was Eleanor, whom he called Tussy. He often said "Tussy is me". With his approval Eleanor took, as a common law husband, Edward Aveling, a friend of Mrs. Besant, leading personality of Theosophy. Like Satanists, he lectured on subjects like "The wickedness of God": unlike atheists they do not deny the existence of God, except to deceive others, they believe in God, but describe him as wicked. Aveling advocated the right to blaspheme.[12]

Karl's favourite son-in-law was one of the main lecturers of a movement which recited poems such as the following:

To thee my verses, unbridled and daring,

Shall mount, O Satan, king of the banquet,

Away with thy sprinkling, O priest and thy droning,

For never shall Satan, O Priest, stand behind thee.

Hail, of the reason the great vindicator,

Sacred to thee shall rise incense and vows!

Thou hast the god of the priest disenthroned.[13]

Such poems were recited in Karl's home.

The connection between Marxism and Theosophy is not accidental. Theosophy has spread to the West the Indian doctrine of the non-existence of the individual soul. What Theosophy does by persuasion Marxism does by force. It depersonalises men, seeking to change them into robots submissive to an all-powerful state. Further light on this subject may be got from a letter written to Karl by his son on March 31, 1854. It begins with the startling words: *"My dear devil."* Who has ever known of a son addressing his father like this? Yet that is how a Satanist writes to his beloved one. Also significant is a letter addressed by his wife to Karl in August 1844: "Your last pastoral letter, high priest and bishop of souls, has again given quiet and peace to your poor sheep."

Marx had expressed his desire in **The Communist Manifesto** to abolish all religion, which one might assume would include the Satanist cult. Yet, his wife refers to him as high priest and bishop. Of what religion? The only European religion which has high priests is the Satanist one. What pastoral letters did he, the man believed to be an atheist, write? Where are they? There remains a part of Marx's life which has remained unresearched.

Richard Wurmbrand demonstrates that many of Marx's associates, such as Engels, Bakunin, Proudhon and Moses Hess, and many of those who put his programme into practice, such as Lenin, Trotsky, Stalin and Mao Tse Tung, were also Satanists. His summing up of Communism is accurate and appropriate:

It is essential to state emphatically that Marx and his confreres, while anti-God, were not atheists, as present day Marxists describe themselves, that is, while they openly denounced and reviled God, **they hated a God in whom they believed.** *His existence is not challenged. His supremacy is .... The ultimate aim of Communism in conquering new countries is not to establish another economic system: It is to mock God and praise Satan.*

This then may throw some light on what follows regarding the life of Karl Marx.

1 Archive for the History of Socialism and the Workers Movement 1925 in German.
2 Marx and Engels, Collected Works, Vol. 1.
3 MEGA L/2 P.164
4 Karl Marx, Collected Works, Vol. 1.
5 Isaiah 14:13
6 2 Chronicles 11.15.
7 Karl Marx "Spielman" (The Prayer) 57-58.
8 Karl Marx "Oulanem" MEGA 1, i (2) 68.
9 *Ibid.*
10 The 18th Brumaire, Karl Marx.
11 "Oulanem."
12 The Life of Eleanor Marx by Chushichi Tzuzuki, Clarendon Press, Oxford, 1967.
13 The Prince of Darkness (quoted in it) by F. Tatford, Bible and Advent Testimony Movement.

CHAPTER 4

Karl The Man

We know from his University records that Karl was a frustrated poet, and because he failed to make the grade, turned in bitterness to philosophy. In that subject he hoped to become a Professor at Bonn University. Again he was disappointed, only falling back on journalism as an outlet for his anger and frustration. In his first year at Bonn his ego had suffered a severe assault. A professor, criticising an essay which Karl submitted for his final examination, noted that the student fell *"into his usual mistake — an exaggerated search after an unusual and metaphorical mode of expression. Therefore the whole presentation .... lacks clarity, often even accuracy."* Rather than profit from what was intended as constructive criticism, Karl became bitterly antagonistic towards the professor. And his worried father was to say to him: *"Unfortunately you are confirming all too well the opinion which I hold of you, that in spite of your many good qualities, egotism is your ruling passion."*[1] Even he himself was to say in a rare moment of honesty of his poetic writings: *"The emotions are generalised and formless .... there is nothing natural .... rhetorical reflections instead of poetic thoughts .... everything is made out of thin air."* Karl did not try to correct his faults, but turned instead to philosophy.

The "Doktors' Klub" was a talk shop where a group of coffee house "intellectuals" met informally. Here Karl became an instant success. Here his ego thrived on the flattery of its members. Here also he was advised to apply to the University of Jena, where things were so lax, a degree could be obtained by correspondence, for he had so neglected his studies he had no hope of getting one in Berlin.[2] Having been rejected as a poet the Club gave him the opportunity to indulge the one subject in which he excelled, disputation.

What Karl probably did not realise is that he was being watched and assessed for future use by agents of conspiracy. Those astute plotters saw in the domineering, opinionated and obstinate young man the right kind of raw material to promote the revolution they had been planning since the 1770's. He was being watched and guided by skilled masters in the art of revolution, and he lapped up the flattery which was so freely heaped on him. Heretofore he had railed against violent revolution, he sneered at radical thugs for their unnecessary use of violence. Socialism was inevitable — that was enough. Now in the hands of master planners of violent revolution he was to become their devoted disciple.

Though flattery was heaped on Karl in the "Doktors Klub" he made very few friends in his whole life, only one lasting friend, Engels. This is not to be wondered at, for he fought with all the socialist writers of the time. Few men were more eloquent in firing abuse at friends and enemies alike. Bakunin, with whom he had long worked, said of him: *"He was a vain man, perfidious and artful."* Schurtz in his reminiscences said: *"I have never seen a man whose bearing was so provoking and intolerable. He had a most obnoxious faculty for seeing the worst in all persons whom he met, and all with whom he quarrelled were denounced in language of unmitigated virulence as traitors or as fools."* Mazzini, the Italian revolutionary, long acquainted with him, said: *"Hatred outweighs love in his heart."* Spargo in his life of Marx gave details of fourteen prolonged and embittered brawls with his fellow revolutionaries. Nesta Webster in **The Surrender of an Empire** says an old socialist, well acquainted with the family, told her no more miserable women could be imagined than Marx's daughters, two of whom, namely Eleanor and Laura and her husband, ended their lives by committing suicide. Eleanor had made a pact with her common law husband, but he backed out at the last minute.

Fritz J. Raddatz's **"Karl Marx. A Political Biography"** was reviewed in the Jewish Chronicle on 13.7. 1979 by Robert S. Wistrich, as follows:

Karl Marx once described himself as a "machine condemned to devour books and then throw them up in different form on the dungheap of history."

His latest biographer, while evidently respectful of the intellectual voracity of this iconoclastic son from a respectable Jewish family, is more impressed by the contradictions in Marx's dictatorial and somewhat megalomaniac personality. We are shown Marx, the man of leisure, indulging his tast for tailor-made suits, choice wines, champagne and caviar, alongside the impatient revolutionary cursing the pharisaic philistinism of his age; we see the impoverished emigre constantly begging his friend, Engels, for more money, and struggling to keep up appearances while denouncing the "Jewish impudence" of his rival Ferdinand Lasalle, whose wealth, fame and social status he bitterly envied. Yet for all his polemical spleen, Dr. Marx was not above having special cards printed to emphasise the upper class origins of his wife, Baroness Von Westphalen.

Raddatz's Marx emerges as an elitist, bourgeois snob rather than the greatest revolutionary thinker produced by the modern labour movement. The champion of the proletariat neither knew nor cared much for workers in the flesh, indeed, he never set foot in a factory. He was an intellectual, Bohemian misfit under capitalism, and one wonders how his aristocratic life-style would have fared under the aegis of drab, puritanical twentieth-century communism.

There is much that is entertaining and amusing in this down-to-earth attempt to demystify the towering figure of Marx. Yet Raddatz ultimately fails to explain why just this hypochondriac, self-hating descendant of generations of Rabbis, so decisively changed the political history of our times. His portrait of Marx is less a political biography than a polemical debunking of the private man — a case-study of the revolutionary as intellectual neurotic and authoritarian petty bourgeois.

Robert Miller, in an article in the Daily Telegraph of 15.4 1981 entitled **"The Unacceptable Face of Marx"** writes: *Among many other undesirable traits in the character of Karl he despised both Jews and Negroes and for a time opposed the emancipation of American slaves on the grounds that it would slow down the revolutionary developments — not, it* *should be said, from the unfortunate Negroes but from the white working class. And if he despised Jews and Negroes he had no great opinion of women, by no means an exemplary husband, for many years he left his family in squalor, though he was well qualified to earn a good living for them. And, of course, as we know, he fathered an illegitimate child by his maid, Helene or Lenchen, while passing off paternity on Engels, who complied, as always, with his every whim. According to the "Economic and Philosophical Manuscripts" of 1844, Marx claimed that bourgeois marriage made women the property of their husbands. But, as with all private property, Marx thought that the owners ought to be expropriated and their property nationalised. This, as Marx declared, would make all women prostitutes. "In the same way as women are to abandon marriage for general prostitution, so the whole world of wealth, that is, the objective being of man, is to abandon the relation of exclusive marriage with the private property owner for the relation of general prostitution with the community." Such was to be the status of women under Communism. He believed there were reactionary peoples as well as classes, and that they would both disappear in a series of horrifyingly destructive wars. Revolution and civil war he thought were both necessary to usher in the new age. On this point he had no illusions about what to expect saying: "We have no compassion and ask no compassion from you. When our time comes we shall not make excuses for terror .... there is only one way in which the murderous death agony of the old society can be shortened and that way is revolutionary terror."*

It is this claim rather than ridiculous racial theorising which makes him still one of the greatest enemies of civilization.

Marx hated his fellow socialists because of their wealth, which humiliated him, and because, with the exception of Engels, they hesitated to throw any of it at him. This infuriated him. Karl broke with Ruge, fought with Feuerbach and Bruno Bauer. He was put out of action by Proudhon.

Ruge, in a letter to his mother about Marx, quoted by Raddatz, says;

*"I am more and more convinced that arrogance and malice
are driving him mad and furious. He cannot tolerate my name
preceding his on the title page. He cannot bear having my
name quoted with his, even though I have, to a certain extent,
after all, made him known to the public. The most idiotic
thing is that I should be held bound to risk my fortune to re-
start the review ...."*[3]

Karl built up his books by laborious research in the
British Museum, but later investigators have discovered that
he plundered wholesale from other writers without acknowledgement, dishonestly passing off huge chunks of their
writings as his own. Dr. K. Menger and Prof. Foxwell in
"The Right to the Whole Produce of Labour" (1899)
showed in detail his wholesale stealing from the treatises
and pamphlets of Ricardo, McCullagh, Hall, Owen, Thompson,
Hodgekin, Gray, all without acknowledgement, and often
with unscrupulous distortion to make them fit his argument.
Professor Hearnshaw says it is hard to avoid the conclusion
that Marx knew the fallacy and even the absurdity of the
theories he propounded in his books, and that he deliberately wrapped them up in ambiguous words to prevent
others seeing through them. Dr. Bohm-Bauwerck, a well-
known European economist, similarly expressed the opinion
that Marx's books obviously consisted of matter put
together as artifical support for views previously arrived at
on different grounds altogether.

A former Jewish Bolshevic Commissar, Morris Gordin,
told how he came to see that the whole Marxist theory is a
fake. Mr. Gordin, after acting as editor of the Communist
organ in America, went to Russia in 1921 and was chief of
the Communist Press Bureau in Moscow until 1924. He told
the Union League of Michigan in an address delivered in
Detroit on January 16, 1931, that he there discovered that
Marx and Engels had concocted their theories first and then
in after years hunted around for facts to fit them. *"My Com-*

munism", he said, *"dropped down dead on the spot."*

Did Marx really care about his fellowmen? Hardly! for in the year 1865 between one legacy and another he inherited nearly £2,000, an enormous sum in that day and age. Did Karl go around to some debtors' prison and offer to restore some poor devil to his family by paying off the debt, or did he even bring a basket of food to some hungry family in the London of the time? Nowhere will one find an account of any such act of kindness. Indeed, with all the money that passed through his hands, he left his own family in want much of the time. Even his own father, who loved him dearly, said in a letter to him that he felt sorry for Jenny, and that she was from time to time a victim, against her will, of a kind of fear, heavy with foreboding, that he could not explain.[4]

When the time came to get married Karl made sure he married no ordinary girl, but an aristocrat, whose family enjoyed a large secure income from its property. And when it was time for his daughters to get married, he became the Victorian father without whose consent they could not decide. He certainly did not want any member of the proletariat for a son-in-law. As for so many of his well-heeled, well-educated followers, the workers were all right to write about but marrying one, well, that would be marrying beneath one, wouldn't it? Karl wrote the following letter to Paul Lafargue on 13 Aug. 1866. It speaks for itself:

London 13 August 1866

My dear Lafargue,
Allow me to make the following observations:

1. If you wish to continue your relations with my daughter, you will have to discard your manner of "paying court" to her. You are well aware that no engagement has been entered into, that as yet everything is provisional. And even if she were formally your betrothed, you should not forget that this concerns a long-term affair. An all too intimate deportment is the more unbecoming in so far as the two lovers will be living in the same place for a necessarily prolonged period of purgatory and of severe tests. I have observed with dismay your change of conduct from day to day over the geologic epoch of a single week. To my mind, true love expresses itself in the lover's restraint, modest bearing, even diffidence regarding the adored one, and certainly not in unconstained passion and manifestations of premature familiarity. Should you plead in defence your Creole temperament, it becomes my duty to interpose my sound sense between your temperament and my daughter. If in her presence you are unable to love her in a manner that conforms with the latitude of London, you will have to resign yourself to loving her from a distance. I am sure you take my meaning.

2. Before definitely settling your relations with Laura I require a clear explanation of your economic position. My daughter believes that I am conversant with your affairs. She is mistaken. I have not raised this matter because, in my view, it was for you to take the initiative. You know that I have sacrificed my whole fortune to the revolutionary struggle. I do not regret it. On the contrary. Had I my career to start again, I should do the same. But I would not marry. As far as lies in my power I intend to save my daughter from the reefs on which her mother's life has been wrecked. Since this matter would never have reached its present stage without my direct intervention (a failing on my part!) and without the influence of my friendship for you on my daughter's attitude, a heavy personal responsibility rests upon me. As regards your present circumstances, the information, which I did not seek out but which has reached me nevertheless, is by no means reassuring. But to proceed. Concerning your position in general, I know that you are still a student, that your career in France has been more or less ruined by the Liege incident, that you still lack the language, the indispensable implement for your acclimatisation in English, and that your prospects are at best entirely problematic. Observation has convinced me that you are not by nature diligent, despite bouts of feverish activity and good intentions. In these circumstances you will need help from others to set out in life with my daughter. As regards your family I know nothing. Assuming that they enjoy a certain competence, that does not necessarily give proof that they are willing to make sacrifices for you. I do not even know how they view your plans for marriage. I repeat, I must have definite elucidation on all these matters. Moreover, you, as an avowed realist, will hardly expect that I should treat my daughters's future as an idealist. You, a man so practical that you would abolish poetry altogether, cannot wish to wax poetical at the expense of my child.

3. To forestall any misinterpretation of this letter, I can assure you that were you in position to contract marriage as from today, it would not happen. My daughter would refuse. I myself should object. You must be a real man before thinking of marriage, and it will mean a long testing time for you and for her.

4. I should like the privacy of this letter to remain between our two selves. I await your answer.

Yours ever,

Karl Marx[6]

This then is the one who is sometimes preferred to Christ, the God-Man, who chose to be born in a stable and to die on a cross between two thieves.

Christ, the God-man, worked with his hands until he was thirty years old, thereby sanctifying manual labour for all time.

For Karl all that mattered was the collective about which he could write. For Christ it was the individual that mattered. *"Amen I say to you rather than scandalise one of these my least ones, it were better for a man that a millstone be hanged around his neck and he drowned in the depths of the sea."* He came to call sinners to repentance. To the woman caught in adultery he would say *"Is there no one left to condemn you, then neither will I. Go, sin no more."* And for the Prodigal Son, there was the fattened calf, rings on his fingers and sandals on his feet. The Good Thief would hear the consoling words: *"This day you will be with me in Paradise."* For the sick He had compassion. He cured the lame, the blind and, in an instant, the lepers. He felt ingratitude: *"Were not ten made clean, where are the nine?"* He raised people from the dead, the widow's son of Nain, and his own friend, Lazarus. He fed the four thousand who were hungry with five barley loaves and two fishes.

"I am the light of the world," He said, *"He who follows me can never walk in darkness; he will possess the light which is life." "Believe me before ever Abraham came to be, I am." "Greater love than this no man hath, that a man lay down his life for his friends." "I am the Good Shepherd, the Good Shepherd lays down his life for his sheep." "Come to me all you that labour and are heavily burdened and I will give you rest. Take my yoke upon yourselves, and learn from me; I am meek and humble of heart; and you shall find rest for your souls. For my yoke is sweet and my burden light." "This then is to be your prayer, Our Father in Heaven, hallowed be your name, your kingdom come, your will be done, on earth as it is in Heaven; give us this day our daily bread; and forgive us our trespasses as we forgive them that trespass against us; and lead us not into temptation, but deliver us from evil. "Your Heavenly Father will forgive you your transgressions, if you forgive your fellowmen theirs; if you do not forgive them, your heavenly Father will not forgive you your transgressions either."* And He died crying out *"Father, forgive them, for they know not what they do."*

1 Marx Heinrich Letter 2/3/1837 to Karl MEGA.
2 Karl Marx, Man & Fighter. Nicolaievsky.
3 Raddatz. P.61
4 MEGA Letter 2/3/1837 1,1/2,P.205.
5 Nicolaievsky. P12.
6 MIML. A German version of the French original appears in MEW.

CHAPTER 5

28 Dean Street, Soho, where Marx lived from 1850 to 1856.
Photograph taken about 1905.

The Years of Poverty

If there is any one thing that has helped to canonize Marx in the minds of his followers it is the legend of his poverty. Why should Karl of all people live in poverty? His education alone would have enabled him to find a number of well paid jobs. The trouble with him was that he did not want to work for a living. As a result, his family suffered much in those London years. His wife made many complaints in letters to friends, once going so far as to say she would be better off dead.

To see Karl's poverty in the context of the time it is necessary to enquire into the wages then prevailing and to set that against the income which he did receive as recorded in letters and other records.

Professor Bowley has estimated that in 1860, the income of an agricultural laborer in the lowest ten per cent of the British population was about £30 annually. An average income for a worker would have been about £45 per annum and for those in the upper ten per cent of the population, a £70 figure would have been typical.

In 1861 nearly a quarter of the male and over one-third of the female population of England and Wales were illiterate, while the professional classes represented under 3 per cent, considerably less than the proportion of paupers. In every trade nine-tenths of the workers were unskilled with an earning capacity that rarely reached 20s. a week; the Scottish miner (with a family of above the average of six children to support) earned 24s.; the Manchester carpenter 28s.; and the craftman in the London building trade 32s. The living conditions were atrocious. According to an address given by Joseph Chamberlain, then Mayor, on 15 January 1875, the average age at death of the Manchester upper middle class was 38 years, while the average age of the labouring class was 17; while in Liverpool those figures were represented as 35 against 15. It thus appeared that the well-to-do classes got a lease of life which was more than double the value of that which fell to the lot of the less favored citizens. This was quoted by Marx in **Das Kapital**.[12]

In the light of this background it is well to see just how poor the Marx family were in those days. In July 1869, Engels settled his accounts with his firm, paid off all Marx's debts and settled an annual pension of £350 on him. Yet Marx claimed that his large sum was not enough for him to live comfortably. A year before, in a letter to Kugelmann he had written: *"You may be sure that I have often discussed leaving London for Geneva .... here I have to spend from £400 to £500 annually; in Geneva I could live on £200."*[2]

Karl was singularly favored when it came to receiving legacies. Always when things were desperate some relative was sure to come to the rescue, and of course there was the never-failing Engels who contributed enormous sums down all the years that Marx spent in London. If the family of the upper ten per cent could live on £70 per annum where then did the vast sums that Karl received go? Robert Payne's biography[3] tells us that in a letter to his uncle, Lion Philips, Karl announced (June 1864) that he had made £400 on the stock exchange. On July 4th he wrote to Engels, asking for the final settlement of the Wolff legacy: *"If I had had the money during the last ten days, I would have been able to make a good deal on the stock exchange. The time has now came when with wit and very little money one can really make a killing in London."*[4]

Marx's income, using Professor Bowley's estimates, was some five times greater than the upper ten per cent of the British laboring classes. Using the 1867 figures presented in that year by R. Dudley Baxter to the Statistical Society of London, we find that Marx's income placed his family in the top 120,000 families in England and Wales. Some 5.1 million families lived below Karl's "poverty line". After 1869, Marx's regular annual pension placed him in the upper two per cent of the British population in terms of income.

Marx felt he was unable to live comfortably on an income greater than that enjoyed by ninety-eight per cent of his countrymen — in a nation which, *per capita,* was the wealthiest in the world.[5] Yet one biography describes Karl's financial problems thus: *"But his anxieties only really ended in 1869, when Engels sold his share in the cotton mill and was able to make Marx a definite, if moderate, yearly allowance."*[6] As Orwell would say, some are more equal than others. It all depends on who writes the history.

In **Poor Karl, The Myth of Marx's Poverty** Gary North concludes his essay thus:[7] *Karl Marx set the pattern, both intellectually and financially for today's young 'Mustang Maoists'. On the dole for most of his life, he spent his days criticizing the very economic structure which permitted him his leisure time. He attacked 'bourgeois liberalism,' yet it was that system of liberal thought which gave rise to an atmosphere of intellectual freedom, without which he would have been imprisoned, and his books burned as a lesson for others. In short, Marx did his best to undercut the very foundations of his own existence. An economist who could not economise, a philosopher who used philosophy as a weapon instead of a tool for contemplation, Karl Marx was ultimately suicidal — economically, politically and intellectually.*

1 Das Kapital 3rd German edition 1881.
2 Marx to Kugelmann 17/3/1868. Letters to Kugelmann 1865.
3 Robert Payne, Marx, Simon & Schuster, 1968, Pp 78-79.
4 Payne P. 354.
5 Baxter's figures appear in The Economic History Review, Vol. XXL (April 1968) p 21.
6 Nicolaievsky & Maenchen-Helfen, Karl Marx P. 234.
7 Published in American Opinion, Belmont, Mass.

CHAPTER 6

Georg Wilhelm Friedrich Hegel

The Dialectic

According to Marx it is only out of the clash of opposites that progress can take place. He had been a student of Hegel who taught quite simply that conflict creates history.

In Hegelian terms an existing force, the thesis, generates a counterforce, the antithesis. Conflict between the two forces results in the forming of a synthesis. Then the process starts all over again: Thesis versus antithesis results in synthesis, going on and on.

What Marx did was, to apply Hegel's dialectic to matter. Mao Tse Tung was to say *"there is nothing in the world only matter in motion"*. Marx claimed to have 'discovered' a scientific law that would explain the history of the world up to his time and for all time to come. This was the law of dialectics applied to history, called dialectical materialism. This 'law' of dialectics has been a major factor in enabling the Communists to defeat their opponents time and time again.

The essence of the philosophy of dialectical materialism is that all development and progress in human society and in nature stems from conflict. Class warfare, for example, is inevitable, and an essential part of the progress towards communism. The true Communist must not only accept the 'revelation' of dialectical materialism, he must also learn to think and act dialectically, so that he is working with reality. To the Communist the only absolute reality is the inevitability of the Communist victory — everything that advances that victory is moral and justified. The Communist claim is that as they discovered the laws governing all development, then these laws become the custody of the Communist Party, which must use them to gain and to hold Communist power.

The word 'dialectic' was first coined by the Greeks, who used it to describe the art of discourse and rebuttal; it was taught that by one person making a statement and another person making an opposite statement it was possible to see two contradictory views on any subject more clearly. A greater understanding of truth to both opponents became possible. Hegel took up this idea of using dialectics in the world of ideas. He believed that dialectics produced a much more developed idea.

Hegel taught that the thesis contains within itself its opposite and he terms the development of this the antithesis. The antithesis is not a mere negation of the thesis, but in fact must contain some truth because of its attack on error in the thesis. Out of all this comes the synthesis, which then becomes the thesis of a new idea. If this is a 'scientific law' as is claimed, why must it suddenly end when the Communist state is reached? Communists shy away from answering *why*? though Hegel, from whom Marx borrowed the idea, taught that dialectical development in the field of ideas would go on indefinitely.

For Hegel it was the idea that was composed of contradictory elements. For Marx it was matter that was composed of contradictory elements.

Truth is absolute, whatever Hegel or Marx might think or say. The synthesis need by no means be any closer to truth than the thesis or antithesis. the truth lies above the two extremes, not between them. In every extreme there is a wandering away from the truth into error. Although the reciprocal extremes seem to be completely antagonistic, they actually share the same crucial error. The true position differs from both extremes smuch more than they differ from each other.

For Marx matter was self sufficient: there was nothing beyond or external to matter. Its contradictory nature provided it with a motive force of development. This would dispose of the necessity of any Cause external to itself. This was Marx's way of abolishing the concept of God.

Why then, it may be asked, with such an inflexible law built into nature, is it necessary for Communists to go to such lengths to make what for them is inevitable come true?

In **"How to be a Good Communist"** Chinese Lin Shaochi asks[1] *"Can Communist Society be brought about?"* *"Our answer is Yes! About this the whole theory of Marxism —Leninism offers a scientific explanation that leaves no room for doubt."* It is this "scientific explanation" based on the philosophy of dialectical materialism which Communists use to justify whatever has to be done to help advance Communism. Lying, cheating, murder are all moral if such things advance the Communist cause.

In **The Programme of the Communist International**[2] we read: *"The conquest of power by the proletariat does not mean peacefully capturing the ready-made bourgeois state machinery by means of a parliamentary majority .... The conquest of power by the prolectariat is the violent overthrow of bourgeois power"* and Stalin in **The Problems of Leninism**[3] says: *"What is the meaning of the possibility of the complete and final victory of socialism in a single country without the victory of the revolution in other countries? It means the impossibility of having full guarantees against intervention, and hence against the restoration of the bourgeois order, without the victory of the revolution in at least a number of countries. To deny this indisputable fact is to abandon internationalism, to abondon Leninism."*

George Orwell called Dialectics double-speak. Now ponder the following reply of Mao Tse-Tung when asked *"what then is Communism, democracy or dictatorship?"* his reply: *"These two things, democracy for the people and dictatorship for the reactionaries, when combined, constitute the people's democratic dictatorship."* A story is told that someone once approached the Duke of Wellington saying *"Mr. Smith, I believe,"* to which Wellington replied: *"If you believe that you will believe anything."*

Contradictions are the essence of Dialectics. Communists are taught to think dialectically, something incomprehensible to the man who uses his commonsense. And because Communists are taught to think dialectically they are taught that to advance is to take a zig zag route to any objective, because progress is made through opposites, advance and retreat. One of the principal Communist textbooks is Lenin's **One Step Forward, Two Steps Back.** In China school children are actually taught to do a dialectical march, taking three steps forward and two steps back.

The American writer, Fred Schwartz, compares the Communist advance to that of hammering in a nail. Anyone who only sees the backward motion of the hammer would find it hard to understand that the backward movement was necessary for the driving in of the nail, but when he sees the backward swing as a portion of a complete process he realises that the withdrawal is as important as the downward thrust to the realisation of the objective. The communists have a slogan which says *"Nature acts dialectically."* This Dr. Schwartz illustrates as follows in **"You can trust the Communists to be Communists,"**[4] *"Wishing to advance dialectically in a room full of people, I do not walk through the aisle and straight toward my goal. Nor do I move slowly through the crowd shaking hands with friends and acquaintances discussing points of interest, gradually nearing the objective. The dialectical pathway is different. It consists of a resolute forward advance followed by an abrupt turn and retreat. Through a series of forward-backward steps the goal is approached. To advance thus is to advance dialectically."*

Their goal is fixed and changeless. It is nothing less than the subjugation of the whole human race to their dictatorship, and they are moving as determinedly towards that goal when they are moving in the opposite direction as when they are moving towards it. Diplomats who do not understand the Communist 'law' of dialectics are wasting their time going to summit meetings with trained Communists. Every now and again we are told that Communism is mellowing — such a phase represents the backward swing of the hammer.

That Dialectics promotes war is borne out by the following statement from Stalin in his **Problems of Leninism:** *"We are living not merely in a state, but in a system of states, and the existence of the Soviet Republic side by side with imperialist states for a long time is unthinkable. One or other must triumph in the end. And before that end supervenes, a series of frightful collisions between the socialist Republic and the bourgeois states will be inevitable."*

Kruschev is especially remembered for his saying that when *"We have ceased to be Marxist-Leninists, shrimps will have learned to whistle."*

American writer, Eugene Lyons, has commented as follows on dialectical materialism:

"Dialectical materialism, whatever else it may be, is the smuggest and most convenient philosophy ever adopted by a ruling caste to its political needs. It finds a bogus consistency in the most startling inconsistencies. There is something monstrous in a dialectical materialism which exploits in order to end exploitation, which flouts elementary human values in the name of humanity, which fortifies new classes to achieve a classless society; which, in brief, presumes to be as heartless as history, instead of opposing its dreams and its hopes to history's heartlessness."

When Bukharin, the Communist theoretician, was concerned that the state was not withering away, but was, in fact, growing stronger, Stalin had him shot. Stalin claimed that this fact was in reality dialectical proof that it was withering away.

Eric Butler in his **Dialectics** says: *"A dedicated Communist may be said to suffer from a form of insanity in that the theoretical concepts he holds are a greater reality to him than the evidence of facts. Dialectical Materialism enables the Communist to murder, lie, betray, to claim that which was black yesterday is white today. But the Communist does not believe that he is murdering or lying or being treacherous. So long as he is advancing Communism he is in fact acting morally because to the Communist the only morality is that* *which advances Communism."*

Morris Hilquit in his **Socialism in Theory and Practice,** writes: *"All factors which impede the path of its (socialism's) approximate realisation are anti-ethical or immoral; contrariwise, all factors or movements which tend in its direction are ethical."*

Lenin stated bluntly: *"The dictatorship of the proletariat is nothing else than power based upon force and limited by nothing — by no kind of law and by absolutely no rule."*[5] and he adds *"Proletarian morality is determined by the exigencies of the class striggle,"* which is another way of saying that the dialectical tactics to be used at any one time depend upon the circumstances. There is only **one** absolute; Communist victory is inevitable. This is, of course, in the future, the Communists' pie in the sky. When all power has been seized by the Communists all will be sweetness and light; not only will there be a new type of society, there will be a new type of human being with no hang-ups and no more tendency to evil. We are not told how this is to be brought about. We must accept on faith that it will happen. This is the great secret that Marx claimed to have discovered.

All over the world there are freedom fighters who are told by their masters that colonies must be free — that is free from Capitalism — but united under Communism. Lenin in true dialectical fashion explained it thus: *"We preach separation although evolution is towards the fusion of nations .... for the same reason that we preach .... the dictatorship of the proletariat, although all evolution goes towards the abolition of the domination of force of one part of society over the other."*[6]

Are Communists nationalists or internationalists? Mao in fine dialectical style says: *"As to whether or not we are nationalists, I can state the following: we are nationalists in as much as this is necessary to develop among our people a healthy socialist patriotism, and socialist patriotism in its essence is internationalist."*[7]

"Democracy" is a much abused word. It has one meaning

in the West, but quite a different meaning in Communist countries. There it does not mean free elections. In his **Foundations of Leninism**[8] Stalin quotes Lenin's view in **The State and Revolution,** that *"the dictatorship of the proletariat is the rule   unrestricted by law and based on force — of the proletariat over the bourgeoisie ...."* and states that the first conclusion to be drawn from this is that: *"The dictatorship of the proletariat cannot be 'complete' democracy, democracy for all, for the rich as well as the poor; the dictatorship of the proletariat 'must be a state that is democratic in a new way ...."*[9]

To all who believe in the pursuit of truth words have a very definite meaning, but terms like "justice", "peace", "freedom", "progress", "welfare of the people", etc. have a very different meaning for the Communist, for to him the ultimate truth is the will of the communist Party, nothing else. Because the end justifies the means, whatever advances the Communist cause is truth, is moral, and this extends all the way to war, despite the fact that Communists are forever talking about peace and peaceful co-existence, or "competive co-existence" as Kruschev called it. In Communist dialectics war is thus a peaceful process, the means to a peaceful end.

In Eric D. Butler's **Dialectics** we read;

"Words become weapons to the Communist. Because his basic philosophy provides him with complete freedom of movement, he can support **even at the same time** *two conflicting opposites — providing that this will advance Communism,* "the will of history". *All agreements are regarded from one viewpoint only:* will they advance Communism?". To the complete Marxist-Leninist, every question must be answered against the background of whether or not it will advance Communism. The Communist mind is not immoral, it is amoral. If it were immoral, there would be a starting-point to reach it. But a mind which not only rejects all concepts of fixed moral precepts, but which can make anything moral which advances the Marxist "revelation", cannot be reached

within the thought forms of the West. Most discussion, Summit Talks, etc. are therefore not only a waste of time, but foster the dangerous delusion that it is possible to reason with the Communists. The only starting point for realistic talks would be an attack on the basic Communist philosophy of dialectical materialism. But there does not appear to be one Western leader capable of doing this. Rather do they reflect the general ignorance of the problem confronting the West by clinging to the hope that if the West can at least maintain its military defences, Communism will become "different".

In the Communist world every crime in the book has been explained away as conforming to the iron law of the dialectic. They include lying, cheating, and murder, including the mass murders of Stalin. He was no sooner dead than Kruschev called him the greatest mass murderer in history, and in the next breath he defended Stalin for being a good Marxist-Leninist.

The theory of dialectical materialism is such a negation of truth any fair-minded person can only conclude that Marx concocted it deliberately to deceive even the elect. The tragedy is that millions, very many of them idealistic young people, really do believe the false prophets who preach this gospel, and follow them unthinkingly as the children followed the Pied Piper of Hamelin.

We know from Karl's beliefs that he was no atheist. He **knew** that the world and each one of us would relapse into the nothingness from which we came if the Creator for a moment withdrew His sustaining hand.

"God is, and at the beginning of time He created the heavens and the earth." (Gen. 1:1). Before this there was no "space" and no "time". Apart from God there was literally nothing (no-thing). Creation was unique. It was not a rearranging or shaping of pre-existing matter of some kind. It was creating out of nothing. *"I beg you, child, to look at the heavens and the earth and see all that is in them; then you will know that God did not make them out of existing*

things; and in the same way the human race came into existence." 11 Mac. 7:28. And in Heb. 11:3 we read "through faith we perceive that the worlds were created by the word of God, and that what is visible came into being through the invisible." Man did not, and could not, make himself, his very being is a gift of the Creator. We are all God's property, more than the clay belongs to the potter, for the potter did not make the clay — he only shaped it. "Friend, who are you to answer God back? Does something moulded say to the moulder: 'Why did you make me like this?' " (St. Paul, Rom. 9:20)

We are made for a purpose, as is all creation. The universe is suffused with meaning and significance. It is no random collection of atoms; each atom of creation is meaningful with a divinely ordained purpose for its being. The simple cell, the smallest form of microscopic life, is more complex than any man-made thing, such as the Eiffel Tower or indeed the city of Paris itself, with all its complexities and ramifications. In the human body billions of cells die and billions of cells are born every minute.

Against this marvel of creation Marx would have us believe there is nothing, only matter in motion. We are expected to take on trust that the world began with an explosion, familiarly known as the "Big Bang"; from that came order, every atom following minute and complex laws with exact clockwork precision, and all this without the aid of any lawmaker. Can there be a law without a lawmaker? We are not told what was there before the "Big Bang", or why it occurred. Such teaching would make orphans of us all, and the earth one big, cold and heartless orphanage.

What a joy to know that each one of us **belongs,** and that we are loved with an infinite love. Who but the God of all knowledge could say: "Yet not a single sparrow falls to the ground without your Father's consent. You are worth more than many sparrows. Every hair of your head has been counted, so do not be afraid of anything." (Matt. 10:29-31.) Who but God could claim to know the number of hairs on your head? .

Take away the God of Love who made us in His image and likeness, and anything goes. Good and evil are what any person thinks they are. Each person would make his own book of rules for living. If each made his own book of rules for the road what chaos there would be! Five hundred years before Christ the Greeks taught that there were natural laws that transcended human understanding, but that we had better obey them or pay the price for disobeying. The Communists have tried to stand nature on its head, for which the whole human race is paying.

1 "How to be a Good Communist" P.38.
2 "The Programme of the Communist International". N.Y. 1936 P.36.
3 "The Problems of Leninism". P.66.
4 "You can trust the Communists to be Communists". P.153.
5 Complete Works, Vol. 18. P.361
6 Quoted by Milovan Djilas, Lenins et Les Rapports Entre Etats Socialistes, Paris, Le Livre Yougoslave, 1949. P.111.
7 On Nationalism and Internationalism, address given before the Slovene Academy of Arts and Sciences, Nov. 16 1948. P.14.
8 "Foundations of Leninism". P.43.
9 Lenin, Selected Works, Vol. 7.P.34

CHAPTER 7

MANIFESTE DU PARTI COMMUNISTE
par Karl MARX et Fr. ENGELS

РУССКАЯ СОЦІАЛЬНО-РЕВОЛЮЦІОННАЯ БИБЛІОТЕКА
Книга Третья

МАНИФЕСТЪ

КОММУНИСТИЧЕСКОЙ ПАРТІИ

Карла Маркса и Фр. Энгельса

ПЕРЕВОДЪ СЪ НѢМЕЦКАГО ИЗДАНІЯ 1872.

СЪ ПРЕДИСЛОВІЕМЪ АВТОРОВЪ

Prix 1 Fr.

ЖЕНЕВА
Вольная Русская Типографія
1882

The Manifesto

Karl Marx's reputation stands or falls on the **Manifesto.** Few people ever read **Das Kapital.** Fewer still understand it. The **Manifesto,** however, is claimed to be the world's greatest best-seller, outselling the Bible.

The **Manifesto** was no spontaneous eruption on the part of Marx following his earth-shattering discovery that there is nothing in the world, only matter in motion. Karl Marx was commissioned by a group calling itself "The League of the Just" to write the **Manifesto.** It was the work of both himself and Engels. All the ideas contained in it had been tossed around for more than seventy years. They originated with Adam Weishaupt, founder of the Illuminati, in the 1770's. He it was who claimed for the first time boldly and aggressively that the end justifies the means. The League of the Just were Weishaupt's men. Marx and Engels were engaged to bring all those ideas together in language that would appeal to, and stir up, the masses. In this field Karl was a master.

The **Manifesto** is made up of ten steps, each destined to lead mankind into a veritable heaven on earth.

The family is the cornerstone of society. If there were no family units there would be nothing to live for, yet Karl would abolish the family and make women the property of the state to be nationalized. Strange proposal from one so close to his own family.

Religion, Karl claimed, was the opiate of the people.

It should not be necessary to refute such an extraordinary statement except to mention a tiny fraction of things produced by religious inspiration. The great Cathedrals and Monasteries of Europe were built mostly by volunteer labour; were the volunteers under the influence of opium? Did St. Thomas More lay his head on a block because he was drugged? St. Augustine was to say: *I have sucked the juice of every pleasure, oh, vanity of vanities, all is vanity,"* and again *"If I have achieved anything, it is because I have stood on the shoulders of giants."* Did he need opium to write his **Confessions** and the **City of God?**

St. John Bosco, a contemporary of Marx, was born in 1815 of poor parents in Northern Italy. While Karl spent his days plotting revolution and the shedding of rivers of human blood, laying down his socialist laws, John Bosco was begging and building, collecting together the stray waifs of society. First they came in ones and twos, then in tens, in hundreds, and eventually in thousands. To stray waifs, without home or parents, he became father. He sheltered and fed them, educated them and gave them skills so they could earn a living. Today his followers are fanned out over the whole free world, wholly dedicated to the same high ideal.

Today in Bombay for instance, just one of Don Bosco's sons, Father Maschio, in voluntary exile from his native Italy since he was 15, looks after the following: In one Boys' Home alone, 1,500 boys rescued from the streets, are looked after. In his St. Joseph's Home, newborn children, found abandoned on the pavements, and even in the dustbins of the city, are taken in. In St. Catherine's Home, nuns who are supported by Fr. Maschio have saved the lives of 4,000 children. Boys from his home are given trades, so that they are sought after because of their skills. Out of 200,000 lepers in Bombay, Fr. Maschio provides food, medicine and other care for 8,000 of them. This is the work of just one John Bosco religious house in just one city. The pattern is repeated wherever there is need the world over.

Mother Teresa of Calcutta, better known over here, does the same kind of work. Who would accuse her of doing such heroic work because she was under some kind of spell?

One commentator has remarked that in India he found missionaries from every denomination binding up the wounds of the old and the sick and all the outcasts of society, but nowhere did he ever come across a Socialist binding up anyone's wounds. They like to make laws which they would compel others to keep, but not for them to touch lepers and the army of the destitute.

Marx recommended the centralization of credit in the hands of the state by means of a national bank with state capital, giving it an exclusive monopoly. Monopoly means power, power over people. Banking is for the experts. This would mean giving the experts a monopoly. This was what was called for by the League of the Just who employed and paid Karl to write the Manifesto. The power they wielded they wanted made absolute. Since the foundation of the Bank of England in 1694, following on the heels of the Battle of the Boyne, the secret societies had been in the business of making governments their pawns by foisting on them their loans at high interest rates. Centralisation of credit would mean absolute financial power for those secret societies.

Next Marx advocated a heavy progressive or graduated income tax. One asks: to what purpose? Why, but to service the huge debts Karl's paymasters intended to create and to fasten on the backs of the workers.

It should be noted that the productive system is so dynamic, thanks to the ongoing perfecting of all kinds of machinery, even to the silicon chip, that all our requirements could be met by the work force working say two or three days a week. No need for workers to work late hours or to take two jobs, or for wives and mothers to be torn from their families, just to earn enough to make ends meet. At least two days work per week are now worked by the work force just to pay the taxes, to pay Karl's heavy progressive or graduated income tax. Somehow the dynamism of the machine had to be combatted. What could be better than a heavy, progressive or graduated Income Tax? It means everyone works for the State, and on everyone there's a file, a very subtle but powerful version of the police state. And all the effort goes to pay interest on money that cost originally just the paper and ink on which it was written.

Marx wanted all property of every kind vested in the

State. Then to what purpose, may one ask, the heavy progressive graduated Income Tax? Where does it go? Who benefits? Marx knew, but he had prostituted his talents and wrote what he was directed.

Marx wanted the property of all emigrants and rebels confiscated. As an emigrant and a rebel himself, one wonders how he would have reacted if some piece of property of his was confiscated in his native Germany, or even that of his many relatives on whom he kept a close eye to see what he could inherit, for inheritance was very dear to Karl's heart.

Karl would have the means of communication and transport in the hands of the State. This is straight out of Weishaupt's Illuminati program. Just fancy every newspaper and magazine, every radio and T.V. station run by the State. Is this not mind control? Is this what free men desire? *"Give me freedom or give me death"* was the cry of American patriot, Patrick Henry. Karl would take away from all others the freedom which enabled him to say what he liked in the Britain where he had unlimited freedom, and where he could live among the upper ten per cent of the inhabitants without ever doing a day's paid labor.

Karl advocated equal liability of all to labor and the establishment of industrial armies, especially for agriculture. Imagine the one who steadfastly refused ever to do a day's paid labor to support his family, wanting to enlist the rest of mankind, both men and women, in a vast industrial army, to go where sent, and to do whatever work assigned, no matter how distasteful or unsuitable to the individual concerned.

The secret societies had been planning bloody revolution in a thoroughly organised way since Adam Weishaupt founded the Illuminati. Karl's task was to provide theoretical justification for the conquest of one country after another by methods of unprecedented barbarism, and the establishment in them of regimes based on slavery, terror and atheism. He talked about the inevitable forces of history bringing about certain results, but in every country where the results he postulated were brought about they did not just happen. They were brought about by the deceit and terror of a small clique of highly trained men skilled in the art of revolution, who had access to unlimited funds supplied by the descendants of Karl's paymaster.

The Manifesto is a direct extension of the diabolical scheme set in motion by Weishaupt in 1776. By examining the Illuminati's secret documents, which were discovered by the Bavarian government, Karl Marx emerges as exactly the kind of character prescribed by Weishaupt for use by, and acceptance into the inner circle of, his great conspiracy. This was to bring about what he called a new World Order. This meant nothing less than complete control over the whole human race. And for this Weishaupt insisted that the end justified the means. To this end both religion and national life must cease to exist so as to *"make of the human race one good and happy family"*.

Weishaupt had been to school with the Jesuits. Recognising the efficiency of their methods, he decided to imitate them, while proposing to himself views diametrically opposed. He said: *"What these men have done for altars and empires, why should I not do against altars and empires? By the attraction of mysteries, of legends, of adepts, why should I not destroy in the dark what they erect in the light of day."* Adepts would be initiated step by step into the higher mysteries — and the greatest caution would be exercised not to reveal to the novice doctrines that might be likely to revolt him .... Nor must antagonism to religion be admitted. Rather Christ was to be represented as the first author of Illuminism.

When the adept was initiated into the higher grades he was told the whole secret of the Order. Part of the discourse read: *"Behold our secret .... If in order to destroy all Christianity, all religion, we have pretended to have the sole true religion,* **remember that the end justifies the means,** *and that the wise ought to take all the means to do good which the wicked take to do evil."*

The aims of the Illuminati can be summarised as follows:

1 Abolition of Monarchy and all ordered Government,
2 Abolition of private property,
3 Abolition of inheritance,
4 Abolition of patriotism,
5 Abolition of the family (marriage and all morality) and the institution of the communal education of children,
6 Abolition of all religion.

This formed a programme unprecedented in the history of civilization.

Of the **Manifesto** Prof. Hearnshaw says:

"It held out a prospect of revenge, destruction, and sanguinary devastation — the overthrow and humiliation of thrones, aristocracies, and above all the hated bourgeousie — that appealed with irresistible attraction to the passions of envy, hatred and malice which filled Marx and his associates with fanatical and diabolical fury. The energy and vigour of the Communist **Manifesto** is the demoniac energy of the madman, possessed by the evil spirits of jealousy, greed and lust for power, and the insane hunger for revenge in respect of imaginary wrongs"

Marx's **Manifesto** and that of Weishaupt are so nearly identical there can be no doubt in any reasonable person's mind that Marx was employed by the Illuminati to write the **Manifesto.**

Marx's liaison with the Illuminati is rarely mentioned because of course the foremost aim of secret society within secret society is to remain secret. These people do not want to make headlines. Such trivia are left to their pawns.

The Rev. Clarence Kelly in **"Conspiracy against God and Man"**[1] says *"Except for certain modifications dictated by changing conditions in the economic and political realms, one could accurately say that Weishaupt was a Communist in the modern sense of the word. But given the sequence of events, it is more proper and accurate to say that Communists are Illuminists — as we shall see when we examine and compare Illuminism and Communism in relation to the nature of*

Government on three essential points of doctrine that lie at the hearts of these ideologies. Non-essential incidentals to the contrary notwithstanding, we shall see that the identity between Illuminism and Communism shows them to be one and the same ideology.

The three points of doctrine are:

1 Anarchism, i.e. the theory that government is by nature intrinsically evil and should not exist.

2 Totalitarianism, i.e. the theory that it is essential to establish a universal dictatorship in order to bring about the condition wherein all civil and ecclesiastical authority will cease to exist.

3 The "withering away" of the dictatorship, i.e. the theory, fabricated for propaganda purposes, that the totalitarian dictatorship will automatically wither away when all governments are under control, and all advocates of legitimate civil authority, along with the remnants of their influence, are exterminated."

In the 1872 edition in German of the Communist **Manifesto** Marx and Engels wrote:

The Communist League .... which could of course be only a secret one under the conditions obtaining at the time, commissioned the undersigned (i.e. Marx and Engels), at the Congress held in London in November, 1847 (while it was still a secret society), to draw up for publication a detailed theoretical and practical programme of the party. Such was the origin of the following Manifesto, the manuscript of which travelled to London, to be printed a few weeks before the February revolution.

And in the Introduction to the Communist **Manifesto**[2] quoting Marx we read:

"The Manifesto was published as the platform of The Communist League .... (which was) before 1848 unavoidably a Secret Society."

Why then is Marx portrayed as the Father of Communism, and lauded in all Communist literature as being a great original thinker?

1 "Conspiracy against God and Man". P.195.
2 N.Y. Washington Square Press 1971.P.21.

CHAPTER 8

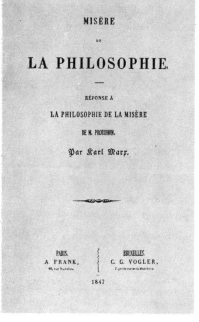

Title page for the book *The Holy Family*

Cover of the book *The Poverty of Philosophy*

The Proletariat

Marx had a pipe dream. He and only he could change human nature, because only to him was revealed the shattering knowledge of dialectical materialism. *"Workers of the world unite, you have nothing to lose but your chains."* **'The Manifesto.'** He would unite the proletariat, and let them become dictators. Fatten human beings up like prize animals; then all would be sweetness and light. But even Prof. Laski has remarked that the history of the human race did not begin and end with the belly.

Trotsky has described how this dictatorship works. Of its nature it must be and is of one man, with a limited sharing of power with a handful of others, as in the Politbureau in the U.S.S.R.

Marx could not but have known that he was planning slavery. But he had his suspicions about the British. He didn't trust them to fall into line. He said the British would never make a revolution, that foreigners would have to make it for them. If only the ghost of Marx could today take a flying visit around Britain. There he would find that the proletariat has become a huge middle class living in homes boasting the kind of comforts even his rich relations in their day would have envied. They drive fine cars and travel agents do a thriving business jetting them like swarms of ants to the sunny Mediterranean for most of the year. There they live it up: they sun themselves, smoke cigars, and wine and dine in the best hotels. Karl's rich relatives never knew anything like it.

How did it come about? It came through the dedication of gifted men who have sat and still sit, at their drawing boards, striving to take the burden of manual labor off the backs of men, and by the pressing of a button to let the machine instead do the work. The machines they invent and perfect have brought freedom and leisure to countless millions, bringing them creature comforts undreamt of by even the upper classes a few generations ago. This is as true of all the developed Western nations as it is of Britain. The workers have thrown off the chains of want without any help from Karl Marx. It is only in the Marxist paradise that the workers have nothing to lose but their chains.

If the workers of the West have to work many hours when they would rather go fishing, it is to pay the taxes levied on them as interest on loans which cost only paper and ink and the salaries of clerks, levied by the same paymasters who paid Marx to write the **Manifesto.** Such manipulation is the confidence trick that dwarfs the sum total of the confidence tricks of all the ages. But for such taxes, the workers of the West could provide for all their needs with perhaps two days work per week. The rest goes to pay the unjust taxes. Well could Rothschild the first say: *"Let me create a nation's money, and I care not who makes its laws."*

Now that his gang create and control the world's money, we see with what disastrous effects on the people of the Third World, where the exports of those poor people can't even cover the interest they have to pay on loans — loans that are nothing more than an entry in a ledger.

There is no longer a proletariat as such in the developed West, just one huge middle class, embracing laborers, artisans and professionals; sure there are differences in their incomes, but the plumber can be, and often is, better off than the professional. There are also some very poor and some very rich, but neither is numerically great. But the very poorest do not starve, as they do in Communist countries such as Ethiopia.

By contrast, in every Communist country a small clique at the top has everything, special shops, special schools, reserved holiday resorts, every privilege known to corrupt man when he gets total power. In every Communist country, the rest cannot even call their souls their own. So much for liberty, equality, fraternity. Lyons says: *"While ordinary mortals queue up for hours to obtain some of the everyday necessities, the new aristocrats shop at leisure in special stores stocked with the best the country produces and imported goods. While top officials and managers draw hundreds of rubles a month — plus an array of perquisites like chauf-*

feured cars, choice apartments — millions on the nether levels struggle to survive on the legal minimum .... In factories and institutions the dining rooms are socially graded: first rate for the important people, third-rate for the workers. Trains have three or four classes .... The best hospitals are reserved for the 'best people.' The upper classes have their status symbols: private suburban houses built on public land, co-operative apartments in town, cars, refrigerators, and other products in short supply, tailor-made clothes — all hopelessly beyond the great mass of the population. They take their vacations as a matter of right in elegant resorts, where a token number of skilled workers gain access only as rewards for outstanding achievement. Even enrollment in higher educational institutions is easier for the children of families with political pull or money bribes to get around academic standards for admission. Then there are what might be called the collective status symbol of the state .... Subways are as ornate as palaces .... The worker goes from the luxurious marble underground station to his shoddy one-room apartment or his verminous slum. Against a background of poverty and weariness, spectacular Sputniks trumpet to the world the might and modernity of the new overlords .... To the normal mind a classless society means political, economic and social equality. But in the U.S.S.R. the very principle of equality is taboo: **'a piece of petty bourgeois stupidity, worthy of a primitive sect of ascetics but not of a socialist society organised on Marxian lines.'** *The words are Stalin's and still express official doctrine."*

British Labour Minister, George Bevin, after a visit to Russia had this to say: *"The inequalities, the unhappiness and the oppression just can't be hidden or ignored .... there is a bureaucratic minority that is extremely comfortably off by any standards."* Lyons adds that there are expensive restaurants in the bigger cities that are filled with well-dressed men and women, paying prices that automatically bar the ordinary mortal .... oases of abundance and swank in a desert of drabness and want.

Christian Rakovsky, a supporter of Trotsky against Stalin, said: *"By means of demoralising methods, which convert thinking communists into machines, destroying will, character and human dignity, the ruling circles have succeeded in converting themselves into an unremovable and inviolate oligarchy, which replaces the class and the party."*

According to Djilas, the disillusioned Yugoslav Communist, one would have to reach back to ancient Egypt fifteen centuries B.C. for a comparable system. He says: *"The communists did not invent collective ownership as such, but invented its all-encompassing character more widely extended than in earlier epochs, even more extensive than in Pharaoh's Egypt."*

Lyons concludes: *"Since Stalin's ukase against* 'rotten-liberal equality' .... *a new class, snobbish as well as arrogant, rules the roost, and below it are other classes, hoping and intriguing for the same comforts and advantages that have moved mortal man since the beginning of time. Only in the lowest depths, in penal camps and exile regions, among the lowest-grade* **kolkhoz** *workers and unskilled laborers, is here a certain equality, the kind Dostoievsky talked of through one of the characters in his novel* **The Possessed:** 'All are slaves and equal in their slavery .... Slaves are bound to be equal."*

CHAPTER 9

Manaqua Cathedral—Nicaraqua poster is of Sandino.

Fr. Miguel D'Escota, Minister of Foreign Affairs, "About Marxism, I think of it as being one of the greatest blessings on the churches, Nicaraqua and the world." May 12, 1980.

Humberto Ortega, Minister of Defense, "Our doctrine is Marxism-Leninism." August, 1981.

Marxism in the Church

Marxism has taken root within the Catholic Church and is now known as Liberation Theology, or the theology of liberation. It is preached on a wide front, but in Latin America and some Third World countries it is also put into action.

Theology, strictly speaking, is the study of God and all things related to Him under the light of divine revelation. Liberation in this sense means being freed from sin. It means salvation and redemption. In the Biblical and the logical sense "liberation" means freedom from the power of sin, Satan and death. Its meaning is religious and spiritual, not political.

However, those within the Church who preach what has become known as liberation theology very cleverly changed the meaning of both words. For them "theology" is very far removed from the study of God. It means instead rational analysis, using the so-called scientific concepts of Marxism, of the economic, political and social situation, in particular of the people of Latin America. Christian words are used, but their "theology" studies, not God, but man.

The religious transcendent sense of avoiding sin and saving one's soul in the case of each individual is not mentioned. These theologians are talking about politics, on which they have taken a very definite stance. They want the destruction of capitalism, which they see as the major evil in the world, and the establishment of socialism.

In this their understanding of either socialism or capitalism is shallow indeed. They do not appear to see that there is a world of difference between international finance monopoly "capitalism" and the free enterprise system of producing goods. Both the socialists of all Communist countries and international finance "capitalists" want the very same thing, monopoly, no competition. They want the power to keep all competitors out of their way. This is a far cry from the butcher, the baker, the grocer, the draper, the farmer, the manufacturer owning his own business and in fair competition producing what is required by the consumer.

In their preaching the liberationists lump all these together with the multi-billionaires of international finance capitalism. Either they do not see, or they turn a blind eye to, the role of credit creators. First poverty is fostered and then supposed to be alleviated by the granting of massive loans at high interest rates, which compounds the poverty.

As churchmen it is strange that they do not mention the social teaching of the Church, that great body of teaching issued by successive Popes that would have solved the various social problems if it had ever been taught and implemented. The tragedy is that it was filed away. Why? As the gospel says *"an enemy did this"*, the enemy within, the Trojan horse in the City of God. The enemy knew it could never take the Church from without, for the history of the Church is the history of strength through persecution.

The preachers of liberation theology say the enemy is capitalism, which they do not define. But free enterprise, healthy competition, is as far removed from monopoly capitalism as it is from socialism. And they take good care not to mention that Communist states everywhere have been set up with monopoly capitalist funds by rich men who knew what they were doing.

But Liberation Theology, like Marxism, is opposed to private productive property, profit and entrepreneurship. Those who preach it do not believe in individual freedom, which must be sacrificed for the good of the "people", but in every socialist country only the people at the top have benefited. Socialism as an alternative to capitalism (not defined) must be established. The Bible must be given a Marxist interpretation. They want the Catholic Church changed, transformed into a "people's" church, in order to join in the fight for socialism. Liberation theology sees the problems of Latin America to lie outside Latin America, namely in the U.S.A.

This cannot be theology, for God is not mentioned. It is ideology. It sees Christianity as nothing more than a vehicle for achieving socialism.

While the action is in Latin America principally, the ideas that inspire it came from Europe. One pundit observed that it carried the tag "Made in Germany". Hegel again!

All this is done in the name of the Catholic Church, their Church. But for some liberationists Jesus is no longer the Son of God, Second Person of the Blessed Trinity. He is reduced to the merely human level and becomes a radical revolutionary in the line of present day Marxist heroes. Yet others see Christ as merely an idea in the minds of the early Christians.

The goal of the Christian then is not the salvation of one's soul, and personal union with God in Heaven, it is rather the establishment of socialism. A new Catholic Church is proposed devoid of metaphysics, transcendence, spirituality, virtues, sanctity, salvation, eternal life. Everything is reduced to politics, the ideology of revolution. There is no mention of the necessity of avoiding sin, to which all men, rich and poor, are prone. For these preachers mankind is divided into two distinct classes, the poor who are good and the rich who are evil. How simplistic.

But Christ came to save all men, the rich as well as the poor. He died for each individual as if he were the only one. Salvation can only come as each individual is converted to the Truth. So instead of the violence of the bomb and the gun, justice and peace can only come to Latin America or anywhere else by converting individuals, of whatever class, that they may come to know the Truth. *"The truth will set you free."*

People who are engaged in violence have no time to think, to reflect. Issues are clouded. Energy is wasted, energy that could be used to build up, not to tear down, for violence begets violence, and the last state is always worse than the first when brought about by violence.

The Church has roundly condemned Liberation Theology in these words:

"The class struggle as a road towards a classless society is a myth, slows reform and aggravates poverty and injustice.

Those who allow themselves to be caught up in fascination with the myth should reflect on the bitter examples history has to offer about where it leads. They would then understand that we are not here talking about abandoning an effective means of struggle on behalf of the poor for an ideal which has no practical effects. On the contrary, we are talking about freeing oneself from a delusion in order to base oneself squarely on the Gospel and its power of realization .... Pastors must look after the quality and content of catechesis and formation which should always present the whole message of salvation, and the imperatives of true liberation within the framework of this whole message ....

"In this presentation of Christianity it is proper to emphasise the transcendence and gratuity of liberation in Jesus Christ, true God and true man; the sovereignty of grace, and the true nature of the means of salvation, especially of the Chruch and the Sacraments. One should also keep in mind the true meaning of ethics in which the distinction between good and evil is not relativised, the real meaning of sin, the necessity for conversion, and the universality of the law of fraternal love.

"One needs to be on guard against the politicisation of existence which, misunderstanding the entire meaning of the Kingdom of God and the transcendence of the person, begins to sacralise politics and betray the religion of the people in favour of the projects of the revolution."

Papal Instruction on Theology of Certain Aspects of Liberation.

One may well ask: How did such a false doctrine take root within the City of God? There is, however, no great mystery if we go back to the last century and see what the secret societies were planning with regard to the Church. The following extracts are taken from the correspondence of the Italian Alta Vendita (or Haute Vente), which is commonly supposed to have been at the time the governing centre of European Freemasonry. The documents were seized by the Pontifical government in 1846. They were communicated by

Pope Gregory XVI to Cretineau-Joly (March, 1846), who published them in his work **L'Eglise en face de la Revolution** with the approval of Pope Pius IX:

"Our ultimate end is that of Voltaire and the French Revolution — the final destruction of Catholicism, and even of the Christian idea. The work which we have undertaken is not the work of a day, nor of a month, nor of a year. It may last many years, a century, perhaps; in our ranks the soldier dies, but the fight goes on ....

"Crush the enemy whoever he may be; crush the powerful by means of lies and calumny .... Let the clergy march under your banner in the belief alway that they are marching under the banner of the Apostolic Keys .... Lay your nets in the depths of the sacristies, seminaries, and convents ....

"It is not in the blood of an isolated man, or even of a traitor, that it is necessary to exercise our power: It is upon the masses. Let us not individualise crime .... It is necessary to generalise it .... Let us not then make more martyrs; but let us spread vice broadcast among the multitude; .... Let them breathe it through their five senses; let them drink it in, and become saturated with it .... Make men's hearts corrupt and vicious, and you will no longer have Catholics .... Draw away the priests from the altars, and from the practice of virtue. Strive to fill their minds and occupy their time with other matters .... It is the corruption of the masses we have undertaken — the corruption of the people through the clergy, and of the clergy by us — the corruption which ought one day to enable us to lay the Church in the tomb ...." Cretineau-Joly, **L'Eglise en face de la Revolution,** pp 120—400.

And in the French Occultist review **Mysteria** of April, 1914, under the signature of Pappus we read:

"Side by side with the national politics of each State, there exist certain obscure organizations of international politics .... The men who take part in these councils are not the professional politicians, or the brilliantly dressed ambassadors, but certain unpretentious, unknown men, high financiers, who are superior to the vain ephemeral politicians who imagine

that they govern the world ...."

The following article is reprinted from **Christian Order,**
published by Fr. Paul Crane, S.J., 65 Belgrave Road, London,
S.W.4, 2 BG.:

*It was first published in China in 1959, entitled "The
Catholic Church and Cuba: A Programme of Action", it was
published by the Foreign Language Press of Peking for "the
exclusive use of the Latin American Section of the Liaison
Department of the Chinese Communist Party."*

*It should be read in the light of the contemporary confusion
within the Catholic Church. The parallel between this comparison and that contemplated in this authentic document is
more than interesting. The text is complete:*

A COMMUNIST DOCUMENT

*"The Catholic Church, whose headquarters is in Rome, is a
reactionary organization which promotes counter-revolutionary activities within the People's Democracies. If the People's
Democracies are to continue to progress towards Socialism
and Communism, they must first and foremost put an end to
the influence of the Catholic Church and the activities which
it promotes. The Catholic Church is not infertile in achieve-
ments, nor is it powerless: on the contrary, its power must be
recognized and a whole series of measures must be taken to
counteract it.*

*Once the political struggle has reached a high degree of
intensity and the forms of production have achieved a high
level of efficiency, we shall be able to destroy the Church. This
is the objective towards which all our efforts are strained. But
if we were to attack it frontally and strike it overtly while we
are still ill-equipped and have not educated the masses pro-
perly, the only result would be to give the Church a still
greater sway over the masses, for then the latter would feel
themselves on the side of the Church and would secretly support its counter-revolutionary activities. We must also avoid
making the counter-revolutionary leaders of the masses
appear like martyrs. The line of action to be followed consists
in instructing, educating, persuading, convincing, and little by*

little awakening and completely developing the political con-
sciousness of Catholics by securing their participation in study
circles and political activities. We must set about the dialecti-
cal struggle within religion through the work of our activists.
We shall progressively replace the religious element by the
Marxist element, we shall gradually transform the false con-
science of the Catholics to the true conscience, so that they
will eventually come round to destroying, by themselves and
for themselves, the divine images which they had themselves
created. This is our line of action in the struggle for victory
against the counter-revolutionary Catholic Church.

We shall proceed to outline a program of the tactics which
have been successfully employed in the Chinese Republic to
liberate the Chinese people from the imperialistic Church of
Rome.

The Church and its faithful adherents must be brought to
play their parts in the regime of the People's Democracy so
that the masses can exert their influence on them. The Church
cannot be permitted to retain its supra-national character,
which places it above and beyond the will of the masses. A
Bureau must be set up within the People's organizations. By
thus imposing the procedure of "democratic centralization" on
the Church, based on the activities of the masses, the way is
opened to bring about patriotic developments which will
weaken the Church and destroy its prestige. This Bureau will
organize national, regional and local associations which will
group the Catholics into patriotic organisms. Each of these
associations will publicly demonstrate its obedience to the
laws of the nation and avow its determination to obey them.

Once these associations have been created and have pro-
claimed their obedience to the laws of the nation, the react-
ionaries will emerge and identify themselves. It is these
counter-revolutionaries who make themselves evident within
the Catholic Church who must first be rooted out firmly, yet
without employing violence. In all cases the measures taken
must be in accordance with the law. The counter-revolution-
aries' aspirations, by their very nature, lead them to actions

against the Government. This principle shows us the kind of laws which must be applied against those who protest. They must be thought as unpatriotic criminals obeying the imperialistic instructions emanating from the headquarters of the Catholic Church, the Vatican.

During this period, the masses will be experiencing a psychological conflict for, on the one hand, they will feel loyalty towards the Church and the Clergy, and, on the other, their patriotism will prompt them to support the People's Government. This conflict must be carefully studied and probed deeply. If precipitate action is taken, without proper allowance being made for the acuteness of the psychological conflict, there is a risk that the Party will be cut off from the masses. If the links between the Church and the masses are very strong, the principle of "two steps forward, one step backward" must be followed. When the People's Government is performing the "one step backward", it must proclaim that it is defending religious liberty, and that it is in deference to the wishes of the masses that it is setting up Committees of reform in the associations, so that the patriotic masses can express their views more directly in the running of Church affairs.

Vigilance is supremely important at this juncture. The Party militants must control the working of the reform Committees and eliminate the reactionaries whom they encounter among the masses. This must be achieved by plugging the following lines: it is patriotic to support the Government and obey the laws; disobedience is unpatriotic; the associations must publicly proclaim their patriotism; unpatriotic elements must be expelled from the associations and tried as criminals by the patriotic masses, for it is the duty of every citizen to punish criminals. The militants must incite the masses against the criminal elements. As soon as the masses have condemned the criminals and expelled them from the associations, they must be tried in accordance with the provisions of the laws of the People's Government. Simultaneously, the associations must renew their public protestations of loyalty to the laws, and take steps to unmask any hidden counter-revolutionaries in their midst.

Although the reactionaries have been unmasked, the psychological struggle within the masses must continue. It is important that the ecclesiastical authorities and the Bishops should assure the masses that religion has became purer as a result of being liberated from criminal and unpatriotic elements. To our Communist militants who are members of these associations falls the important task of bringing the Church leaders to make these declarations. They must also assure the masses that the Government and the Party take their wishes into account in these matters. During this period further disputes will, of course, arise. If arbitrary action is resorted to, we shall lose our control of the masses. The People's Government must ensure that all these disputes are exploited and envenomed to the maximum degree.

During these controversies care must be taken to flush out any counter-revolutionaries who had previously escaped detection. The same watch-words must be observed during this period as during the preceding, viz.: it is patriotic to obey the laws; disobedience is unpatriotic and criminal. The masses must also be kept informed of the results of the negotiations between the State and the Church, as well as of the resurgence of patriotism among the religious masses; and of the fact that this patriotic upsurge is rapidly supplanting their former sentiments. Except in the field of spiritual affairs, any hint or reference to a link with the Vatican must be pilloried and vilified as being motivated by imperialistic interests and supporting counter-revolutionary activities.

The experiences of sister-countries prove that the Vatican will lodge public protests against our campaign. These protests must be utilized as constituting further proofs of the Vatican directed conspiracy of the Church.

This brings us to the next stage of our attack, the objective of which is the destruction of the link existing between the Church and the Vatican. During this attack it is to be anticipated that the clergy will react violently, for they will sense that they are being assailed in their inner citadel and the very source of their power. They must be reminded that their protests against the attacks, to which they are subjected because of their links with the Vatican, are unpatriotic and are in conflict with the laws and the State. They must also be made to feel that they are the embodiment of something unpatriotic. The task of our militants is to convince the masses that individuals can have their own religion without the Vatican having the right to dictate in the affairs of all the Churches in the world. Our militants must also explain the principle of the coexistence of patriotism and religion. In this was the masses are alienated from those who take their cue from the Vatican and the way is opened for the establishment of an independent Church.

A preparatory campaign must be carried through before an independent Church can be publicly proclaimed. Any clerical personalities who have resisted all persuasion to conform to the wishes of the Government will be denounced at gatherings of the masses. Their protests on these occasions will be turned against them to destroy their influence on the masses. The best way to achieve this is the simple tactic of anonymous accusation. Our militants must initiate such denunciations of these clerics and other personalities. History provides innumerable precedents proving the possibility of legal action against those who are opposed to the separation of the Church and the Vatican. During this phase we must accumulate all the arguments necessary to convince the Catholic intellectuals that a break with the Vatican is a step forward and not a step backward. The legal provisions of the Constitution of the People's Republic protecting all religions, and the history of the different Protestant movements, will help to convince these intellectuals. Simultaneously, our militants will have the task of inducing the Catholic associations to unite in a unanimous demand that the People's Government should authorize the setting up of an independent church in order to cleanse the Catholic associations of any unpatriotic stigma caused by a few elements which still cling to the link with the Vatican. The necessary authorization will be granted by the People's

Government, and the independent Church will be organized. It should be borne in mind that the break between the Catholic Church and the Vatican has no importance except for theologians. The masses are but tenuously linked with the Vatican in their religious practices.

We now reach the final stages once the separation between the Church and that Vatican has become an accomplished fact, we can contrive things so that we select those to be consecrated Bishops. This will lead to protest from the Vatican, accompanied by a major excommunication. Those primarily involved in this crisis must be brought to realize that this phase of the struggle takes place at a level far above the rank and file of the faithful. The Catholic associations will continue to function, and the masses will be encouraged to practice their religion within the bosom of the new Church. If this phase of the struggle is conducted with tact and dexterity, the liturgy will not be destroyed and the masses will perceive but few differences in the new Church. The protests of the Vatican against our consecration of the Bishops will percolate only to the Hierarchy of the Church and the People's Government will undertake the responsibility for rejecting the Vatican's protest. We shall thus gradually isolate the "Old Guard" of the Vatican. Once they have been thus isolated, we shall find it increasingly possible to take legal action against them, for they will feel irresistibly impelled to make spectacular protests and play the role of martyrs. As a result of this, they will necessarily compromise themselves by indulging in unpatriotic actions.

Although our struggle against the Catholic Church is by this time already victorious, we must still employ persuasion in dealing with the rear-guard of the clergy. This moderate policy will bring the masses to realise that the People's Government is really concerned to ensure freedom of religion for everyone, and, at the same time, those who protest against its policy are lumped in the category of those who oppose the sentiments of the people and the Government. Once the time comes when the posts of responsibility in ecclesiastical affairs are in our *hands, and their incumbents are docile to the will of the People's Government, we shall proceed to the progressive elimination of those elements of the liturgy which are incompatible with the People's Government. The first changes will affect the sacraments and the prayers. Thereafter the masses will be protected against any pressure or obligation to attend Church services, or practise their religion, or organize societies with some devotional purpose. It is notorious that when the practice of religion becomes simply a matter left to the individual's sense of responsibility, it is gradually forgotten. The rising generations will succeed the older, and the religion will become merely an episode of the past, important only as a topic to be considered in histories of the world Communism movement."*

Lenin had a name for all those who would promote the revolution outside Russia. He called them useful idiots. Among those who preach Liberation Theology there must be many of Lenin's useful idiots, but also many conscious co-operators with the Secret Societies whose purpose is the annihilation of Christianity.

CHAPTER 10

The Russians in Berlin — 1945

How Marxists Take Over

Karl states in the **Manifesto:** *"You must, therefore, confess that by 'individual' you mean no other person than the bourgeois, than the middle-class owner of property. This person must indeed by swept out of the way, and made impossible."*[1] Many contend that Marx did not intend this statement to be taken literally, that he meant the process to be a gradual one. But it cannot be denied that from the time of the take-over in Moscow in 1917 down to the present day in Cambodia the pattern has been the same, wholesale murder of the innocent on a scale unmatched in any previous period of history. Modern weapons have helped the Marxists to do this more efficiently and more quickly than it could ever have been done in the past, but modern weapons do not explain the satanic hatred that has accompanied the slaughter in every country where they have taken over. It was Lenin himself who issued the order on December 25, 1918 that in deciding the fate of any prisoner there was to be no concern whatever about whether the prisoner had ever been active in resistance to Communism. The only question was the economic or professional class to which the prisoner belonged. If he were a small shop keeper, or owned any property, or in any way belonged to the bourgeoisie, he was to be killed at once. The effect of this ruthlessly chilling policy would be to destroy potential resistance for the future. And it gradually did. Lenin, Trotsky and then Stalin consolidated their brutal power until either resistance or escape was almost hopeless. The procedure by which the accomplished these results was cunning, massive and merciless. This was Communism in practice — we now give some case histories, taken from a document called **"What is Communism"**[2], of the methods used in various countries over the last sixty-seven years.

In 1919, Bela Kun set up his Communist regime in Hungary. For many months his two chief lieutenants, Tibor Szamuelly and Joseph Pogany, operated their murder trains throughout the country. These trains, loaded with armed executioners, were sent continuously into one section of the country after another, where as many members of the populace were seized and murdered on the spot as the crew of the train could handle, before moving on to spread their terror elsewhere. Eventually the regime was overthrown, but in the meantime this was Marxism at work, with all its premeditated brutality.

The following episode occurred in the City of Kharkov, in about 1920 or 1921, when Lenin's agents were trying to subjugate the Ukraine so that it could be brought into the USSR when that consolidation of Moscow's Marxist power was put together in 1922. At one point in this subjugation the Communists were thrown out of Kharkov, long enough so that a commission, containing several doctors, was sent into the area by the civilized governments of Europe to find out what had been taking place.

The report of this commission, or extracts from it, were immediately published in Berlin, in the form of a pamphlet with pictures, names, and other facts as certified by the doctors. The whole print run of the pamphlet was then bought up by Communist agents and destroyed. But in the meantime some few copies of the original run had escaped destruction. One was a copy that had already come into the hands of Prince Yusopov. That copy is now in Portugal. The doctors on that commission stated that, in their opinion, the suffering inflicted on those innocent victims in Kharkov was the worst that human beings had ever been obliged to live through.

The women had been stripped completely naked, and tied up, each with her back to a heavy post which had been set in the ground in a flat and wide open space. The most terrible cruelties were then perpetrated on those helpless victims during the days before death finally relieved them of their agony, culminating in this horror of horrors: which is that burning live coals were thrust into their vaginas and kept there, until the fire and the heat had been exhausted.

Ho Chi Minh has been presented, to young people

especially, not just in Communist countries but by the media in the West, as a great hero and a savior of the down-trodden. It was in Hanoi, in 1946, with the aid of United States money, equipment, and moral support, that he made his debut among the mighty. By bribing the Chinese General, and deceiving the French, Ho managed to get his troops established in Hanoi. But there were two small sects of native Vietnamese in that area who had been organised as anti-Communist supporters of Chiang Kai-shek. For Ho they represented a very definite potential danger for the future. They could even become the rallying point for substantial anti-Communist resistance. Ho determined to have the members of these two groups exterminated.

But how? By simple slaughter? Not at all. Routine murder would not have created the proper psychological effect to serve as an adequate deterrent. Ho was smarter than that. He rounded up the members of the two sects, and had them buried separately, upright and alive, in holes dug for that purpose in fields outside Hanoi, so that just their heads were sticking up above the surface. He then had harrows driven back and forth across those fields, to scratch and tear and chop those living heads like so many small tree stumps as the harrows went over them.

Richard Wurmbrand, a Rumanian Baptist pastor, spent 14 years in jail under the communists. One of his many books on his imprisonment is called **Tortured for Christ.** The following is just one paragraph describing just one of a multitude of horrors:

"I have testified before the Internal Security Subcommittee of the U.S. Senate. There I described awful things, such as Christians tied to crosses for four days and nights. The crosses were put on the floor and hundreds of prisoners had to fulfil their bodily necessities over the faces and bodies of the crucified ones. Then the crosses were erected again and the Communists jerred and mocked: 'Look at your Christ, How beautiful He is.' I described how, after being driven

nearly insane with tortures, a priest in the prison of Potesti was forced to consecrate human excrements and urine and give Holy Communion to Christians in this form. All the Biblical descriptions of hell and the pains of Dante's Inferno are nothing in comparison with the tortures in Communist prisons."

William C. Bullitt was America's first Ambassador to the U.S.S.R. In **A Talk with Voroshilov** he relates the following episode which occurred in the early reign of the Communists in the U.S.S.R. At a banquet in Moscow in 1934, Voroshilov told Bullitt that in 1919 he persuaded eleven thousand Czarist officers at Kiev to surrender by promising them that if they surrendered they, their wives and their families would be permitted to return to their homes. When they surrendered, he executed the eleven thousand officers and all male children, and sent the wives and daughters into the brothels for the use of the Russian Army. He mentioned in passing that the treatment they received in the brothels was such that none of them lived for more than three months. Voroshilov believed that in carrying out a crime of such staggering proportions he was merely being a good Marxist-Leninist.

Many times we are told that such things did of course happen in the early days of Communist conquest but that now that it has come of age, so to speak, it is mellowing. This then is what happened in Cambodia less than a decade ago. The leaders of the Cambodian Communist Party, the majority of them, were converted to Marxism while they were students in France. Returning to Cambodia, they organised the Communist Party which they called the Khmer Rouge. They set out to be the best Communists the world had ever seen. They conducted the programs demanded by their Marxist doctrines with an amazing consistency and ruthlessness. These doctrines taught them that the environment generates character, that the capitalist environment generates an evil character, that the cities are the hadquarters of capitalism, that the bourgeoisie must be liquidated and the residual people removed from the capitalist environment of the cities, that physical labour is regenerative.

Translating these doctrines into deeds, they ordered the evacuation of the cities of Cambodia. Everyone had to go. No one was exempt for humanitarian reasons. The people were animals and should be treated like animals. Three million people who were crowded into Phnom Penh were ordered to leave the city one day. Everyone had to leave just as they were. Children in schools were not allowed to go home and join their parents but were driven out of the city like cattle. Hospitals were emptied of doctors, nurses and patients. The situation is described in the book **"Murder of a Gentle Land"**[3]:

"Troops stormed into the Preah Ket Melea Hospital, Phnom Penh's largest and oldest hospital, and shouted to patients, physicians and nurses alike, 'Out! Everybody out! Get out!' They made no distinction between bedridden and ambulatory patients, between the convalescing and the dying, between those awaiting surgery and those who had undergone surgery. Hundreds of men, women and children in pyjamas limped, hobbled, struggled out of the hospital into the streets where the midday sun had raised the temperature to well over 100 degrees Fahrenheit. Relatives or friends pushed the beds of patients too wounded, crippled or enfeebled to walk, some holding aloft perfusion bottles dripping plasma or serum into the bodies of loved ones. One man carried his son, whose legs had just been amputated. The bandages on both stumps were red with blood, and the son, who appeared to be about twenty-two, was screaming, 'You can't leave me like this! Kill me! Please kill me.' "

The population of Cambodia was about 7 million. It is estimated that between two and three million died. The remainder were forced to engage in the physical labor necessary to grow rice. The number of dead did not trouble the Communist leaders, and Ieng Sary, their foreign Minister, said *"As long as we have one million left, that will be enough to make the new man."*

Dr. Schwarz in **Why Communism Kills, The Legacy of Karl Marx,**[4] says, *"Pol Pot and his associates have earned the right to be called the most consistent Marxists the world has ever seen. In the Communist program for human regeneration, killing is as necessary as the fire of the furnace is for the creation of steel. This program of slaughter is rational if the basic premises of Marxism are accepted. If there is no God who teaches, 'Thou shalt not kill,' and if people are merely animals, why should they not be treated as animals. Husbandmen who breed finer animals and destroy the inferior ones in the process are respected and honoured throughout the world. The Communists believe that they are the husbandmen who have been selected by history to enact the programs that will result in the creation of perfect human animals. To hesitate to eliminate the diseased would be to betray their mission."*

Antonov Ovseyenko, whose father led the Bolshevik storming of the Winter Palace in 1917, has recently published the book entitled **"The Time of Stalin — Portrait of a Tyranny"**. He calculates those killed as a result of the Communist conquest of Russia at 100 million.

In China Mao Tse-tung formally decreed that a hundred million Chinese were to be murdered. One can only conclude from the number of refugees fleeing the country that the process of liquidating so many is still at work. If anything, the Chinese are the most expert of all in ways of inflicting torture and murder. And all these horrors are perpetrated in the name of Marx and Lenin.

In the developing western countries like the U.S. and Britain, the technique is somewhat different but no less deadly. The following is an extract from the book "The Naked Communist", by W. Cleon Skousen, placed in the United States Congressional Record for 10th January 1963. Mr. Skousen served for several years with the American Federal Bureau of Investigation, and it was through his work that he drew up a list of 45 objectives aimed at political, economic, industrial and moral disruption. Reproduced below are the aims relating to moral disruption. It will be noted that some of the objectives (listed in the order that they appear in the book) have already been reached, while others are objects of campaigns now being conducted by various interested pressure groups.

21.   *Gain control of key positions in radio, television and motion pictures.*

22.   *Continue discrediting (American) culture by degrading all forms of artistic expression....eliminate all good sculpture from parks and public buildings and substitute shapeless, awkward and meaningless forms.*

24.   *Eliminate all laws governing obscenity by calling them "censorship" and a violation of free speech and free press.*

25.   *Break down cultural standards of morality by promoting pornography and obscenity in books, magazines, motion pictures, radio and television.*

26.   *Present homosexuality, degeneracy and promiscuity as "normal natural and healthy".*

27.   *Infiltrate the churches and replace revealed religion with "social" religion. Discredit the Bible and emphasise the need for intellectual maturity which does not need a "religious crutch".*

28.   *Eliminate prayer or any phase of religious expression from schools.*

38.   *Transfer some of the powers of arrest from the police to social agencies. Treat all behavioural problems as psychiatric disorders which no one but psychiatrists can understand or treat.*

40.   *Discredit the family as an institution. Encourage promiscuity and easy divorce.*

41.   *Emphasise the need to raise children away from the negative influence of parents. Attribute pre-*

judices, mental blocks and retarding of children to the suppressive influence of parents.

42. *Create the impression that violence and insurrection are legitimate aspects of the country's tradition, that students and special-interest groups should rise up and use "united force" to solve economic, political and social problems.*

43. *Overthrow all colonial governments before native populations are ready for self-government.*

1 Karl Marx. "Manifesto"

2 Robert Welch. "What is Communism?"

3 "Murder of a Gentle Land" by John Barron and Anthony Paul, published by the Reader's Digest Press. P.17.

4 "Why Communism Kills, The Legacy of Karl Marx". Dr. Fred Schwarz. P.10.

CHAPTER 11

Prime Minister, Winston S. Churchill, left; President, Franklin D.
Roosevelt, center; Chairman, Josef Stalin, right
at Yalta in February, 1945.

The Elite

If there is a Third World War raging all around us today, and many contend there is, then our war is not with the terrorists who throw bombs or hi-jack planes. These are only the useful idiots so described by Lenin, the pawns in the game. The bomb-throwing today is only a small part of the total war raging on the financial, economic and moral fronts.

The crucial issue being fought out with deadly malice aforethought is, whether the state exists to serve the individual or the individual exists to serve the state? When Christ said the Sabbath was made for man he was affirming forever the sacredness of human life, all human life. Marx, the disciple of Hegel, taught the opposite. Hegel taught that the individual has no value, except to fit into society as a functionary. For him the state was God. He said:

"The State is the absolute reality, and the individual himself has objective existence, truth and morality only in his capacity as a member of the State."

But what is the state? What is the Marxist state? According to Trotsky it works as follows: —

The Communist Party dictates to the Proletariat,
The Central Committee dictates to the Communist Party,
The Politbureau dictates to the Central Committee,
Finally the Secretary dictates to the Politbureau.

This Stalin did for thirty years, as did Lenin before him. Lenin said the State was power unrestricted by any law.

When Stalin was opposed by Bukharin and his associates, who pleaded for the adoption of a legal code by which to guide one's actions in the Communist paradise, Stalin rejected their pleas as so much rot and triviality. Bukharin and his associates were at the mercy of the one man who was the law and the state, and eventually Bukharin was disposed of by the firing squad.

Both Lenin and Stalin died in their beds — and all Stalin's successors. This has not happened by chance or by some stroke of luck, for all of them have been no more than frontmen for the real power brokers who make the decisions and are far removed from the public scene. Now and again we are dropped a hint by their contact men, as when President Woodrow Wilson said: *"Some of the biggest men in the U.S. in the field of commerce and manufacturing know that there is a power so organised, so subtle, so complete, so pervasive, that they had better not speak above their breath when they speak in condemnation of it."*

So there we have it. In the words of the President of the mightiest state in the modern world! *"There is a power,"* for whom the Governments, the Presidents and the Stalins of this modern world act out their party piece, even when the party piece demands going to war, as the U.S. president knew so well. He had been elected on the one solemn promise: *"He will keep us out of the war."* And all the time the preparations were being made to get his country into the 1914-18 war.

There was a time when there was a certain amount of mystery in all this, but not any more. There are among us today scholars who seek the truth and are not afraid to proclaim it, whatever the consequences to themselves personally. One such is Professor Anthony Sutton of the Hoover Institute of War and Peace. He has written books such as **"Wall St. and the Bolshevik Revolution," "Wall St. and the Rise of Hitler"** in which he proves there would never have been a Russian Revolution or a rise to power by Hitler if it had not been for the massive funding and giving away of technology, food and raw materials to make war weapons mainly by the U.S. but also by all the developed and rich nations of the West.

Sutton's latest work, written in 1983, is on this power elite. It is called **The Order,** the name of the secret society, the American branch of the Illuminati, founded at Yale when Karl Marx was still in High School. Sutton came upon the list of its members from inception to the present time more or less accidentally, just as the records of the Illuminati were found following an electric storm on the body of a messenger. (They were handed to the Bavarian authorities, after which the Illuminati went underground.) This American branch is known as Chapter 322, and more formally for legal purposes as The Russell Trust. Its members are sworn to secrecy. It has rules and ceremonial just as the parent body in Europe has. It is also known as Skull and Bones.

From the beginning and with great determination The Order set out to control the educational system of the United States. Chosen brethren were sent to Berlin to study the philosophy of Hegel. When they returned The Order saw to it that the purpose for which they were sent to Berlin was realised. Sutton says in **"How the Order Controls Education"**:[1]

"In the 1850's, three members of The Order left Yale and working together, at times with other members along the way, made a revoltuion that changed the face, direction and purpose of American education. It was a rapid, quiet revolution, and eminently successful. The American people, even to-day, in 1983, are not aware of a coup d'etat.

The revolutionary trio were:

Timothy Dwight ('49), Professor in the Yale Divinity School and then 12th President of Yale University.

Daniel Coit Gilman ('52), first President of the University of California, first President of the Johns Hopkins University, and first President of the Carnegie Institution.

Andrew Dickson White ('53), first President of Cornell University and first President of the American Historical Association."

All three went to the University of Berlin. Gilman studied under Karl von Ritter, who wrote the antithesis of Karl Marx's **Manifesto,** (no doubt under direction from The Illuminati,) which later become the foundation of Naziism. There also studied Wilhelm Wundt, the founder of experimental psychology in Germany and the later source of the dozens of American PhD's. who came back from Leipzig, Germany, to start the modern American education movement.

At Berlin were right Hegelians who paved the way for Hitler and left Hegelians who paved the way for Lenin and company. The point to remember is that both groups use the Hegelian theory of the State; militarism, Naziism and Marxism have the same philosophic roots.

Returning to America our trio, promoted by The Order, proceeded from Yale to control the education of America's present and coming generations. We have seen what prestigious positions they were handed. Practically all their professors in Europe were members of the Illuminati whose stated aims regarding education were as follows:

"We must win the common people in every country. This will be obtained chiefly by means of the schools, and by open, hearty behaviour, show, condescension, popularity and toleration of their prejudices which we shall at leisure root out and dispel."

The most promising pupil to arrive on the scene was John Dewey, who was to become the main creator of modern educational theory. The money barons in the guise of their foundations saw to it that Dewey did not lack funds to implement his ideas. They matched together Dewey and all the big guns, Ford, Carnegie, Rockefeller, Peabody and others.

Dewey worked for his doctorate at Johns Hopkins University from 1882-86 under Hegelian philosopher, George Sylvester Morris, who in turn got his doctorate from the University of Berlin. From there Dewey went to the University of Michigan as Professor of Philosophy. In 1894, he went to the University of Chicago and in 1902 was appointed director of the newly founded — with Rockefeller money — School of Education, the University of Chicago itself having been founded with Rockefeller money. The University of Chicago and Columbia Teachers College became the key training schools for modern American education. Dewey became the apostle of social changes. In **My Pedagogic Creed** he states:

"The school is primarily a social institution. Education

being a social process, the school is simply that form of com-
munity life in which all those agencies are concentrated that
will be most effective in bringing the child to share in the
inherited resources of the race, and to use his own powers for
social end. Education, therefore, is a process of living and not
a preparation for future living."

The social end Dewey had in mind was the service of the
state. Like his master, Hegel, Dewey supposed that the
individual has no value except as he or she serves the state.
According to Hegel: *"The State is the absolute reality and the*
individual himself has objective existence, truth and morality
only in his capacity as a member of the State."

Both for Hegel and Dewey, his disciple, the individual has
no rights except to serve the state, and the subconscious
idea all the time is to work towards the world state or total
power for the power brokers who never lose sight of the
main objective.

To achieve world power the power brokers stop at nothing, not even war, and indeed nothing suits them more
than a real hot war. That is why Marx, Lenin, Hitler and
Stalin were all their gifts from their particular kind of gods.

The average person naively believes that war happens
because negotiations break down between nations. They
would not have done much delving into Hegel's "law" of
dialectics and would not realise that the manipulation of left
and right on the domestic front is duplicated in the international field where "left" and "right" structures are
artificially constructed and collapsed in the drive for a one-
world synthesis.

Revolution is presented as a spontaneous uprising by the
poor against an autocratic state. We never hear of the
massive funds that have been poured into every revolution
by the world's richest men. There is now no denying the
part played by the Wall Street banking firms in the Russian
revolution, nor in the financing of Hitler. It is not denied. It
is just conveniently ignored.

The 1939-45 war could be said to be the working out of

the dialectic, Naziism being the thesis and Communism the antithesis. The war ended with a strong America and no one country, or even a collection of countries, able to challenge her. There was grave danger each country would like to go back to minding its own business, so an enemy had to be created to give challenge, and what or who else but Stalin. So the power brokers, mainly resident in the U.S., began the process of building up a great military power in the U.S.S.R., sending massive amounts of food, raw materials and the technology to make the bombs and all else that would keep the ordinary people of the world in a state of perpetual tension. Just as the American educational system could be said to carry the tag: "Made in Germany", the military power of the U.S.S.R. could be said to carry the tag: "Made in the U.S.A." The power brokers keep other pots boiling while all this is going on, in the Middle East, in Africa, in the Far East.

In **"How The Order Creates War and Revolution"** Sutton says: *"The Order must be seen and explained in terms of the Hegelian Dialectic process. Their operations cannot be explained in terms of any other philosophy: therefore The Order cannot be described as "right" or "left", secular or religious, Marxist or Capitalist. The Order, and its objectives, is all of these and none of these.*

Our descriptive world history in the West and Marxist countries consists only of description and analysis within a political frame-work of "right" or "left". For example, historical work published in the West looks at communism and socialism either through the eyes of financial capitalism or Marxism. Historical work published in the Soviet Union looks at the West only through Marxist eyes. However, there is another frame for historical analysis that has never (so far as we can determine) been utilized, i.e. to use a framework of Hegelian logic, to determine if those elites who control the State use the dialectic process to **create** *a predetermined historical synthesis."*

Today the technique for bringing us into their New World

Order, or Orwell's "1984", is called **"Management by Crisis."** According to the **Don Bell Reports,** P.O. Box 2223, Palm Beach, Fl. 33480 it works as follows:

1 The power elite creates, invents, or finds an existing crisis,

2 They widely advertise the crisis,

3 Always citing world renowned academics, they propose their solution to the crisis. This is designed in such a way that at least one of three goals is achieved:

(A) The crisis acclimates the population to the need of a New World Order, and/or

(B) The crisis initiates or expands on the placement of the actual machinery to be used in the New World Order. The machinery may be legislative, corporate, legal, economic and so on .... and/or

(C) The crisis actually helps destroy the present nation-state system.

The current nuclear arms race is one of the most potent tools that these Crisis Managers have to create a state of panic, and they are handling it very carefully to assure its most effective use. There are a number of groups subordinate to the power elite, e.g. The Trilateral Commission, The Bilderbergers, The Council of Foreign Relations in the U.S., Club of Rome, Parliamentarians for World Order, The New Age Movement and many others, all working towards the same end. We are not short of crises, the arms race, Middle East crisis, South African crisis, the economic crisis of unemployment worldwide, terrorist crisis, budget balancing crisis and many others.

When the power elitists have selected a crisis to use, at least three very powerful groups swing into action. The communications media headline and highlight the situation in every possible way in order to stir up popular opposition to the existing situation, or thesis. The tax-exempt foundations which funded Dewey provide the finances, academic "experts" promote the crisis through the schools and universities, and finally the World and National Councils of

Churches convert any political, economic, or social crisis into a moral crisis (as with the present S.A. crisis). Finally, when these "advertising" and propagandising establishments have swung into action and popularised the issue, then there are hundreds of supposedly independent groups that go into action, staging parades, strikes, attacks on institutions, people, even buildings. How such groups are activated and used to create demands for a change that will aid the building of their New World Order is seldom mentioned.

On Nov. 9, 10 and 11, 1984, a "Social Management Seminar" was held at the Washington Hilton Hotel. Attending were representatives of more than one hundred activist and futurist organizations whose various aims are to promote some aspect of the New World Order, called **WorldView 84;** the Chairman was Ervin Laszio, director of the United Nations Institute for Training and Research (UNITAR). Previously he had been project director of the Club of Rome's "Goals for a Global Society". In his opening speech at the **WorldView 84** seminar he said: *"There is evidence that shows that the system that we have put in place since World War II — the global economic and social techno-industrial system — cannot be indefinitely sustained, that in fact it is already on its last legs .... Any straightline projection of present trends finds the world socio-economic system running into the unyielding wall of overpopulation, underdevelopment, polarization: with lines of demarcation widening between rich and poor, East and West, North and South, the city and the countryside. We live .... at the tail end of one world civilization and at the dawn of another .... My main concern is to show that in the coming period of transformation we shall, indeed, have a chance to be* **masters of our destiny."** The call was made to all leaders of the organizations sponsoring the World Future Society to work together to develop the kind of society that would fit into the New World Order. This is called "networking", a system of organization that binds together all of the groups committed to a **New World**

Order in such a way that **most people don't see them or think that they are conspiracies.** If any outsiders become too curious, the network must be set up so that "its center is elsewhere .... and its life does not hinge on any of them," that is, any one of the hundreds of organizations involved in the conspiracy.

Since the present most important "crisis" concerns "the danger of a nuclear holocaust," Robert Strange McNamara, World Bank President (1968—1981), Trilateral Commission Member, director of the World Future Society, sent a special report to the **WorldView 84** symposium, stating among other things that *"nuclear weapons serve no military purpose whatsoever. They are totally useless except only to deter ones' opponent from using them."* Therefore all the activist and futurist groups should continue to promote unilateral disarmament. The World Future Society of which McNamara is a director is one of the most important of all the proponents of the New World Order. Founded in 1966, it has chapters, committees or coordinators in approximately 91 cities of the world, with local groups sponsoring lectures and other activities. Among its publications is **The Futurist,** a bimonthly which claims to have *"the largest circulation of all future-oriented journals .... discusses what actions people may take to improve the future."* One of its articles concerning "crime and public safety" provides an indication of what its real goal is. The article opens thus: *"The adult criminal of the twenty-first century may be less common than his twentieth century counterpart, in part because of the way society treats children from the moment they are born. Parental care in the year 2000 may be different from today's, and better, since by then* **the movement to license or certify parents may be well under way.** *In most cases, certified couples would be allowed to have their own natural children. In some instances, however, genetic scanning may find that some women and men can produce 'super' babies but are not well suited to rear them. These couples would be licensed to breed, but will give up their children to other people licensed to rear*

*them. The couple who raises the child will be especially suited
to provide love and compassion and take the best possible
care that the child feels wanted and needed in society ....
could lead to better development of their egos and, thus,
capabilities. Child breeding and rearing may be considered
too important to be left to chance. This change in attitude will
have a major impact on the criminal justic system in that
wanted children will have fewer environmental reasons to turn
to crime, and* **controlled breeding will result in fewer
biological reasons for crime ...."**

At this **Worldview 84** much time was spent in discussing
economics and finance. The general conclusion: *"It is readily
apparent that we now have a World Economy and we must
form a World Government with enough power to regulate it"*
One speaker pointed out that *"government debts are so out
of control that the entire present economic system must collapse."* Here then is the crisis which must be managed in accordance with the **Management by Crisis** Technique of the
New World Planners. What must be done? The solution:
Developing countries even now do not have sufficient
margins in their balance of trade to make repayment of their
debts .... Eventually the only escape will be default. Loans
subject to default equal more than the new worth of the
entire American banking system. Reverberations from such
defaults will shake the financial structure of the country and
the world. **The World Constitution and Parliament
Association is already in the process of setting up a
Provisional World Government to take over in the
event of the collapse of the global infra-structure.** In
addition, the independent Commission on International
Development Issues, commonly known as the **Brandt Commission** after its Chairman, Willy Brandt, currently head of
the Socialist International, was discussed and approved, as
it has already been approved and promoted by the UN.

All things relating to the creation, establishment and
maintenance of The New World Order (World Government)
were discussed, and plans laid down for promotion and

execution of the various pieces in the plot by the various activist and futurist groups attending this **WorldView 84** symposium. The Heritage Education and Resource Organization, P.O. Box 202, Jarretsville, MD. 21084, has provided the main portion of this information concerning **WorldView 84.** It also states that David Rockefeller's Trilateral Commission and the World Future Society in the main are funded by the same multi-national corporations. **Management by Crisis** is formed by what they call **networking** if you're one of them, and by **conspiracy** if you're one of those who see through them. Barring miracles, we are heading straight for Orwell's "1984".

This then, Marxists would have us believe, is the inevitable working out of the dialectic. In **Das Kapital** Karl posed capitalism as thesis and communism as antithesis. Any clash between these two forces cannot lead to a society which is either capitalist or communist, but one which would be a synthesis of the two. The clash of opposites in the Helegian system must bring about a society which is neither. In the Hegelian scheme of events, this new synthesis will reflect the concept of the State as God and the individual as totally subordinate to an all-powerful State.

Where then do Parliaments come in, in all this? These institutions are there merely to allow individuals to **feel** that their opinions are of some value and to allow a government to use whatever wisdom the "peasant" may somehow have. As Hegel puts it: *"By virtue of this participation, subjective liberty and conceit, with their general opinion, (individuals) can show themselves palpably efficacious and enjoy the satisfaction of* **feeling** *themselves to count for something."*

In **"How the Order Creates War and Revolution"**[1] Sutton comments:

"War, the organized conflict of nations, is only the visible outcome of the clash of ideas. As John Dewey, the Hegelian darling of the modern educational system, puts it:

'War is the most effective preacher of the vanity of all merely finite interests, it puts an end to that selfish egoism of

the individual by which he would claim his life and his property as his own or as his family's."[2]

Of course this war-promoting Dewey paragraph is conveniently forgotten by the National Education Association, which is today busy in the 'Peace Movement' — at precisely that time when a 'peace' movement most aids the Hegelian Soviets."

Seeing the amount of real power the secret societies exercise, especially the American branch known as The Order, and how powerless elected governments seem to be in the face of them, one can only conclude that governments are allowed to exist only as so much camouflage, behind which the Secret Societies hide, and to carry out their orders. Sutton says in **How the Order Creates War and Revolution:**[3]

"In brief, while the U.S. public was being assured by the U.S. Government that the Soviets were dastardly murderers, while 'Reds' were being deported back to Russia by the Department of Justice (in the 1920's), while every politician, almost without exception, was assuring the American public that the United States would have no relations with the Soviets — while this barrage of lies was aimed at a gullible public, behind the scenes the Guaranty Trust Company was actually running a division of a Soviet bank! And American troops were being cheered by Soviet revolutionaries for helping protect the Revolution. That, dear readers, is why governments **need** *censorship. That's why even 50 years after some events, it is almost impossible for independent researchers (not the bootlickers) to get key documents declassified."*

"Revolution is an Art" writes Oldstock Ryder in **The Great Conspiracy,** *"but the Revolutionaries would have us believe that it is a natural cataclysm, as inevitable as a volcanic eruption — a spontaneous uprush of popular revolt against insufferable wrongs .... The art of revolution is that by which a small but well organised minority compels an unwilling but unorganised majority to submit to the overthrow of the State and the dictatorship of a few professional agitators who grasp power in the name of the People. The method remains the same today as it was in 1789-1793."*

1 "How the Order Creates War and Revolution".P.5.
2 John Dewey, "German Philosophy and Politics".P.197.
3 "How the Order Creates War and Revolution".P.66.

CHAPTER 12

Memorial on the grave of Karl Marx,
incorporating the original headstone.

The Legacy of Marx

The Twentieth Century has seen more death by violence than any century in recorded history. The atrocities of Hitler's Germany have been well recorded in books and films, but the evil of Naziism no longer exists. It is dead, yet it is posed as the only evil, the only threat to the peace of the world. Meanwhile the Gulag Archipelago continues to be no less a hell on earth than it was in the Twenties and Thirties. Hitler and Stalin were probably the two greatest tyrants in history, but while Hitler's system is dead, that created by Lenin and Stalin continues, undisturbed by any public outcry from the so-called free world. There is no way this can be understood by anyone genuinely seeking the Truth, except that it is part of a conspiracy. The Power Elite controls the media on a world scale. Little by little, that power is building up a favorable picture of Communism or Socialism, the stepping-stone that inevitably leads to a Communist state. In modern parlance Socialism is the "in" thing. The frightful crimes committed in the take-over of any country by the Communists are played down and then submerged in a welter of unimportant NEWS about sport, the weather, anything at all. Yet the founders of the Communist states have been quite forthright as to the means they would employ to seize power. The Bolshevik programme was, and is, essentially one of murder. There is ample evidence of this from many quarters. In his book **Traitors Within** (1933), former Detective Inspector Herbert T. Finch of Scotland Yard recorded that thirty years previously he had concealed himself in a room and heard Lenin and Trotsky addressing what was supposed to be a meeting of "foreign barbers in London." He heard Lenin declaim:

"It must be bloodshed on a colossal scale .... We must revolt, and when we revolt there shall be no mercy .... In Russia first, and then from one side of Europe to the other .... They must perish, down to the man who keeps a stall in the street".

Trotsky (real name Bronstein) has written a book in

advocacy of terrorism, and when the programme of wholesale massacre was launched in Russia his speech ordering it was thus reported in the **Red Gazette,** official organ of the Red Army, Petrograd, of Sept. 1, 1918:

"We shall harden our hearts into iron, we will temper them in the fire of endurance and in the blood of the enemies of liberty. We will be cruel, hard, pitiless, until we feel no pity and are unmoved by the sight of our enemies' blood. We will drown them by thousands in their own blood. For the blood of Lenin (just wounded by the Jewess Dona Kaplan), Uritzky, Zinovieff, and Volodarshi, let us shed torrents of bourgeois blood, more blood, MORE BLOOD!"

The London Times of September 3, 1922, published a despatch from Riga saying:

"According to Bolshevist figures the Tcheka executed 1,766,-118 persons before being renamed the supreme political administration last February."

The late Lord Sydenham in the House of Lords in 1923 computed the total loss of life consequent on the Russian Revolution by killings, famine and disease, as then in excess of 20 million souls. Many more millions have since been slaughtered and starved to death.

The London **Morning Post** book, **The Cause of World Unrest** (Grant Richards, 1920) quoted extracts from the diary of Ferdinand Lassalle, fellow-socialist and contemporary of Karl Marx, as saying:

"The time will soon be at hand when, in very deed, we will help ourselves with Christian blood."

As time goes on, and as Communism becomes more firmly established in the world, truth becomes more easily suppressed in a welter of propaganda. For instance, in a world in danger of being totally annihilated, we are told by the media that the present ruler of the U.S.S.R. likes western clothes and that recently his wife bought some jewellery in the West with her Access card. So much for Marx's centralization of credit in the hands of the State; whose state? whose world? which few?

While we are regaled with such trivia in the West, the Communist Party rules by establishing and maintaining a total monopoly over every aspect of life, the political, judicial, economic, educational and cultural. The Party formulates all the laws and administers them after they have been passed. It controls the army and the police force. It designs the economic plan of the nation. It controls manufacturing, distribution, banking and trade, so that it monopolises employment. It selects and trains all teachers, prepares the curriculum for all schools, and decides which schools students attend. It organises and controls the labor unions, the news media, artistic and sporting activity. Even religion is subject to the direction of a commissar.

Because of its monopoly, the Communist Party exercises complete power over the life of every citizen. This power is literally that of life and death. The citizen can be arrested and imprisoned with or without trial; he can be executed by judicial or administrative degree; he can be dismissed from his job and made unemployable so that he starves; he can be forbidden to live where he chooses within the country or to travel throughout the country as he wishes; he cannot leave the country without permission, which is rarely given; he is restricted in what he reads, hears and says, so that his mind is deformed through lack of knowledge of the truth, and his personality through suppressed convictions. The Communist dictatorship has been defined as "a society in which the Communist Party can, at will, render any individual unemployable and thereby cause that individual to starve." A citizen in such a society possesses no basic rights. He is a slave. The Communist Party owns him, body and soul, and can dispose of him at will. The only freedom he has is to submit and obey. His only deliverance is in flight. Those who decide to flee must face the Berlin Wall, the Iron Curtain running right down the centre of Europe, and the Bamboo Curtain drawn around China. Millions fled, and continue to flee, from Communist China to settle on the barren hills of Hong Kong. The Vietnamese stood their ground during a thirty-year war, but took to their boats in their thousands to go anywhere, even to the bottom of the sea, in preference to life under a Communist regime. Lenin defined the dictatorship of the proletariat as "the rule — unrestricted by law and based on force — of the proletariat over the bourgeoisie, a rule enjoying the sympathy and support of the labouring and exploited masses"[1] Since the dictatorship is based on force and unrestricted by law, individuals possess no civil rights. The government is unrestricted by constitution or the rule of law. This is naked tyranny. And in the words of Trotsky, in practice the Communist Party dictates to the proletariat; the Central Committee dictates to the Communist Party; the Politbureau dictates to the Central Committee; and the Secretary dictates to the Politbureau.

A familiar ploy to assuage the fears of people in the West is to say that communism is mellowing, that the excesses in the U.S.S.R. in the past were due to the evil character of Stalin. His successor, Kruschev, in a famous speech on the crimes of Stalin to the Central Committee of the Communist Party of the US.S.R. in 1956, lists some of his outrageous crimes. Among these he includes the arrest and execution of 70 per cent of the members of the Central Committee that elected Stalin. He states:

"It was determined that of the 139 members and candidates of the party's Central Committee who were elected at the seventeenth congress, 98 persons, i.e. 70 per cent, were arrested and shot (mostly in 1937-8)."[2]

After describing Stalin as one of the greatest mass murderers in history, saying he was not a reluctant murderer but an enthusiastic one, he concluded by saying *"Don't misunderstand me, Stalin was a good man. He was a Marxist-Leninist. He did these things as a good Marxist-Leninist."* Kruschev could just as easily have said that Stalin was a good promoter of dialectical materialism, or that, as a member of the Illuminati, the end justified the means in everything he did.

Much play is made of democracy by the Communists, but when in the 1920's some such demands were made, a rather candid warning came from Leo Kamenev, one of the founding fathers: *"They say today,"* he argued, *"let us have democracy in the party; tomorrow they will say, let us have democracy in the trade unions; the day after tomorrow workers, who do not belong to the party, may well say, give us democracy too …. and surely the myriads of peasants cannot be prevented from asking for democracy."* This was the logic of totalitarianism. Stalin put an end to the debate once and for all. In defending his "most democratic constitution in the world," he explained on November 25, 1934: *"there is no question of freedom for political parties in the Soviet Union apart from the Communist Party. We Bolsheviks consider this provision one of the merits of the constitutional project."* **Pravda** wrote rapturously, *"What a delight to be able to divide the history of human civilization into two phases so clearly: Before and after the constitution bestowed upon us by the great Stalin."* Nearly all the authors of the constitution, along with the editor of **Pravda,** were duly executed in its name, some of them before the document had been formally adopted.

That the effects of almost unlimited power can corrupt even basically good men is remarked on by the writer Djilas, himself a once enthusiastic member of the Party. Former revolutionary heroes, self-sacrificing and full of ideals, he says *"become self-centred cowards without ideas or comrades, willing to renounce everything — honour, name, truth and morals — in order to keep their place in the ruling class and the hierarchical circle."* The world, he believes, *"has probably never seen such characterless wretches and stupid defenders of arid formulas as they became after attaining power."*

The American writer, Eugene Lyons, went to Russia as an admirer of the socialist ideal. After nearly seven years there as an observer he has this to say in his **"Workers' Paradise Lost",** Paperback Library, Inc. N.Y. *"The best*

*people, by moral criteria, are the most likely to be excluded.
Those capable of applying force without stint, the fanatics and
the sadists, have tended to take over. Soviet history has been
a process of triumph for the most insensitive and egotistical,
the connivers and bullyboys. In a world where questioning
and truth-seeking are crimes, the mediocre have had an
advantage over the brilliant. Among the upper echelon 'establishments' of the world the Soviet is probably the crudest. It
represents the end-product of a struggle for the survival of the
fittest — the fittest for a totalitarian society — and therefore
the most unfit for a humane, civilized society."*

We now live in the 1980's, yet nothing has changed. In
"Murder of a Gentle Land" John Barron tells of the
horror and terror of the seizure of power in Cambodia
where more than one million people, some of the gentlest
and most inoffensive in the world, were brutally murdered.
It is in our day, yet the world has looked the other way, as it
did when the Hungarians and the people of Czecho-Slovakia
tried to free themselves.

Why do the people of the free world look the other way?
Why do they put up with want in the midst of plenty, as if
these monstrous crimes happened in the reign of Ghenis
Khan? Why do they watch their factories close down week
after week and just walk helplessly away from them as if it
were an act of God? Why is there so much industrial unrest,
so many strikes? Why do the workers not know the difference between a just and an unjust strike? The Church has
given the following guide-lines to those who would feel
impelled to go on strike. It is taken from **Christian Order**
for May 1985:

*A strike is in essence a withdrawal of labour, basically
what you might call a negative act. That withdrawal can be
just or unjust. In order that it may be just, there are certain
conditions that have to be fulfilled:*

In the first place, *the cause of the strike must be reasonable; in accordance, that is, with the reasoned judgement of a
reasonable and normal human being. This means that the*

decision to strike must not spring from class hatred, for example, or any other unreasonable motive. Again a trivial motive is excluded as ground for a strike because it, too, is out of accord with sound and sensible reasoning. Men cannot strike justly, therefore, 'just for the hell of it' or because they happen to dislike the boss or, say, his wife. Neither must the strike involve the breaking of terms of a just contract of employment unless those terms have already been rendered void by the unjust action of the party against whom the strike is directed. It is immoral to break one's pledged word. Men cannot strike, therefore, for an increase in their own productivity, except that it be to protect themselves justly and with regard to the public good against any harmful effect on their living standards caused by rising prices.

In the second place, *workers cannot strike justly for a cause which, though reasonable, is of relatively small account by comparison with the harm that will be brought by the strike. There must be an obvious proportion, in other words, between the misery and the suffering — to say nothing of the economic loss — which a strike will bring in its course and in its train, and the cause, even though reasonable, for which men strike. It is exactly the same with any other form of self-defence. I cannot, for example, empty both barrels of a shotgun into a thief who is in the process of lifting 50p from my hall table. His action may justify a kick in the shins, but not a charge of buckshot in the stomach.*

In the third place, *to be just, a strike must have a reasonable chance of success because, once again, the suffering brought on by the strike may well be heavy and men have no right to inflict it on others if the just cause for which they fight has no chance of succeeding.*

In the fourth place, *a strike is a defensive withdrawal of labour. It cannot lend itself therefore, to violence and intimidation — even against the guilty party — evil subterfuge, the scarifying and beating up of innocent third parties in order, thereby, to bring pressure to bear more quickly on an employer. Here, very typically, the end does not justify the*

146

means: these must be themselves just.

In the fifth place *and finally, just because a strike is a serious business, it must be made use of only as a last resort; which means, in fact, that it cannot take place before all reasonable negotiating and arbitration machinery has been brought into play. It is difficult to think of an occasion when an unofficial strike, a lightning strike or a walk-out is ever justified.*

The potential for supplying all that is necessary to sustain life was never so great in the history of mankind as it is today. Yet there were never more strikes, both just and unjust. The just strike occurs because the income workers receive buys progressively less and less. Employers are faced with the same problems, costs are always rising, and as happens so many times, they are eventually forced out of business when they cannot pay their way.

Money is nothing more or less than a symbol by which goods are exchanged. It was invented by the art of man, for the convenience of exchange by serving as a common measure of things saleable. As a **common** measure it ought to be **stable.** *"As a measure used for estimating the value of things,"* writes St. Thomas[3] *"money must keep the same value, since the value of all things must be expressed in terms of money. Thus exchanges can readily take place and, as a consequence, communications between men are facilitated."*

What do we find today? Governments the world over steal, by minting worthless coins, and the only vestige of a standard of value is the note issue of a private bank enjoying monopoly privileges in the U.S. According to St. Thomas it is the duty of the State to see that money or exchange-medium is a stable measure of value. Just as the State must maintain stable measures of weight and length, in view of commutative justice in buying and selling, so it must aim at stability of the price-level, the price of a thing being the expression of its exchange-value in terms of money.

Now what happens when governments surrender their

right to maintain a stable money-unit in the same way that they insist on their right to control weights and measures of lengths Governments become beggars, and the people they represent become no better than slaves. Government Ministers in any country wherever would face a firing squad or a standing army any day rather than face up to the money manipulators and confidence tricksters. Even the richest and most powerful nation the world has ever known, the U.S., meekly submits to this modern form of slavery. President Woodrow Wilson has expressed it thus: *"A great industrial nation is controlled by its system of credit. Our system of credit is concentrated. The growth of the nation, therefore, and all our activities are in the hands of a few men .... We have come to be one of the worst ruled, one of the most completely controlled and dominated Governments in the civilized world — no longer, a Government by conviction and the free vote of the majority, but a Government by the opinion and duress of small groups of dominant men."* Of this group Christopher Hollis says, in **The Two Nations** published by George Routledge & Sons Ltd.[4] : *"Behind the ostensible government,"* in Roosevelt's policy, *"sits enthroned an invisible government owing no allegiance and acknowledging no responsibility to the people."* One could fill a book with such quotations concerning the system as it affects the U.S. and indeed the whole world. The western world is bursting with unsold goods. We are told that man can find no way to distribute them. But man has found a way to go to the moon and to come safely back, yet he looks helplessly at food mountains, knowing not what to do while millions starve. A young pop singer by his efforts collected some millions of pounds — an excellent thing to do to awaken the conscience of the people of the affluent West, but those who create and control the world's money could have done the same long before anyone starved, with one stroke of the pen.

There is a Mafia in the underworld about which the world is told. But the Mafia of the underworld destroy only themselves. They cannot touch those who will not buy their drugs or whatever else they sell. They cannot exact tribute from the man in the street. There is a Mafia of the over-world which can and does exact tribute from the whole human race from the cradle to the grave, by its system of creating and lending what it claims the right to call money, at such high interest rates neither capital nor interest on a world scale can ever be repaid. About 90% of the taxes we pay is their tribute. This oligarchy owes no allegiance to any country. It claims the world as its oyster. It creates and finances revolution and anarchy worldwide, and when the opportune moment comes it sends in its Communist bullyboys to take over.

The reader may well ask, what has this got to do with Karl Marx? This Mafia is the selfsame one that paid Marx and Engels to write Manifesto, and that has ensured it is kept on the best-seller list. Marx had the talents to turn the tables on this Mafia, but he chose to prostitute his talents and to write as they dictated. His link with Satanic worship is the key to an understanding of his writings and of the passionate hatreds he showed towards his fellow human beings. For this war that is raging all around us is above all else a spiritual one. This Mafia and its conscious and uncon-scious co-operators do the work of the Evil One. The ultimate objective is World Dictatorship, what they prefer to call The New World Order, which does not at all sound threatening. It is to facilitate the achievement of their New World Order that we are asked to change our laws, to legalise what is immoral, so that one not-so-fine day every country will have common laws regarding family, health, education, the lot.

A spiritual war can only be won by spiritual means. The Mafia of the overworld, for all its power of taxing and taxing to exact its tribute to make slaves of the whole human race, will in the end be beaten by the little people, those hidden and unknown who do the will of the Father who created them. The human race is a fallen one that has been redeemed. The grace to conquer evil by doing good is there for the asking for all men, by the means of their redemption. The selfsame means were there for Karl Marx, but he chose to betray, not to save. Therein lay his ultimate failure. He was a false prophet whose deathly course became the "Legacy of our times."

1 Problems of Leninism — Moscow: Foreign Languages Publishing House, 1953. P. 51.
2 The Dethronement of Stalin. P. 10.
3 Comment. in Ethic., Lib. V, Lect. IX.
4 The Two Nations. Published by George Routledge & Sons Ltd.P.219.

INTERPRETATION OF ABBREVIATIONS

Mârx, Karl and Frederich Engles, Historisch-Kritisch Gesamtausgabe, Werke Schriften, Briefe, (Complete historical critical edition, Works, Writings, Letters) on behalf of Marx-Engles Institute, Moscow, published by David Rjazanov. (Frankfurt-on-Main: Marx-Engles Archive, 1927). This is MEGA, indicating Section, Volume, Part, and page nos.

Marx, Karl and Frederich Engles, Werke (Works) (Berlin: Dietz-Verlag, 1974). This is MEW. The Volume number is in Roman numerals, the page number is in Arabic numerals.

Marx, Karl and Frederich Engles, Collected Works (New York: International Publishers, 1974). This is CW with Volume and page numbers.

Marx, Robert Payne, (New York: Simon & Schuster, 1968) Cited as Payne.

Marx, Eleanor, Vol. 1 Family Life, 1855-1883 Yvonne Kapp, 1972 Lawrence & Wishart, London. Cited as Kapp.

Marx, Karl, Man and Fighter, Boris Nicolaievsky and Otto Maenchen-Helfen. Cited as Nicolaievsky. Penguin Books.

Marx, Karl, Was Karl Marx a Satanist? Richard Wurmbrand, Diane Books Publishing Co. Cited as Wurmbrand.

Workers Paradise Lost, Eugene Lyons, Paperback Library, Inc. N.Y. Cited as Lyons.

INDEX

Other books by Deirdre Manifold:
Fatima And The Great Conspiracy

RE-ORDER - CORRESPONDENCE

G.S.G. & Associates, Publishers
P. O. Box 6448
Eastview Station
Rancho Palos Verdes, California 90734

CORRESPONDENCE - RESEARCH

Deirdre Manifold
15 Dalysfort Road
Salthill, Galway, Ireland

Wm. H. McIlhany
Individualist Research Foundation, Inc.
P. O. Box 7486
Beverly Hills, California 90212-7486

NOTES

NOTES